Values and Value
Post-Migrant Society

Astrid Wonneberger · Sabina Stelzig ·
Katja Weidtmann · Diana Lölsdorf
Editors

Values and Value Change in the Post-Migrant Society

Editors
Astrid Wonneberger
Department Soziale Arbeit
HAW Hamburg
Hamburg, Germany

Sabina Stelzig
Department Soziale Arbeit
HAW Hamburg
Hamburg, Germany

Katja Weidtmann
Department Soziale Arbeit
HAW Hamburg
Hamburg, Germany

Diana Lölsdorf
Department Soziale Arbeit
HAW Hamburg
Hamburg, Germany

ISBN 978-3-658-45106-6   ISBN 978-3-658-45107-3   (eBook)
https://doi.org/10.1007/978-3-658-45107-3

Translation from the German language edition: "Werte und Wertewandel in der postmigrantischen Gesellschaft" by Astrid Wonneberger et al., © Der/die Herausgeber bzw. der/die Autor(en), exklusiv lizenziert an Springer Fachmedien Wiesbaden GmbH, ein Teil von Springer Nature 2023. Published by Springer Fachmedien Wiesbaden. All Rights Reserved.

This book is a translation of the original German edition "Werte und Wertewandel in der postmigrantischen Gesellschaft" by Astrid Wonneberger, published by Springer Fachmedien Wiesbaden GmbH in 2023. The translation was done with the help of an artificial intelligence machine translation tool. A subsequent human revision was done primarily in terms of content, so that the book will read stylistically differently from a conventional translation. Springer Nature works continuously to further the development of tools for the production of books and on the related technologies to support the authors.

© The Editor(s) (if applicable) and The Author(s), under exclusive license to Springer Fachmedien Wiesbaden GmbH, part of Springer Nature 2024

This work is subject to copyright. All rights are solely and exclusively licensed by the Publisher, whether the whole or part of the material is concerned, specifically the rights of translation, reprinting, reuse of illustrations, recitation, broadcasting, reproduction on microfilms or in any other physical way, and transmission or information storage and retrieval, electronic adaptation, computer software, or by similar or dissimilar methodology now known or hereafter developed.
The use of general descriptive names, registered names, trademarks, service marks, etc. in this publication does not imply, even in the absence of a specific statement, that such names are exempt from the relevant protective laws and regulations and therefore free for general use.
The publisher, the authors and the editors are safe to assume that the advice and information in this book are believed to be true and accurate at the date of publication. Neither the publisher nor the authors or the editors give a warranty, expressed or implied, with respect to the material contained herein or for any errors or omissions that may have been made. The publisher remains neutral with regard to jurisdictional claims in published maps and institutional affiliations.

This Springer imprint is published by the registered company Springer Fachmedien Wiesbaden GmbH, part of Springer Nature.
The registered company address is: Abraham-Lincoln-Str. 46, 65189 Wiesbaden, Germany

If disposing of this product, please recycle the paper.

Contents

Introduction: Values and Value Change in the Post-Migrant Society... 1
Astrid Wonneberger, Sabina Stelzig, Diana Lölsdorf and Katja Weidtmann

Do Egalitarian Attitudes Promote Integration? 25
Silke Hans

Attitudes and Values of Young Men with and Without Migration and Refugee History in Relation to Gender and Equality............. 57
Silke Remiorz, Katja Nowacki and Katja Sabisch

"we've Gotten Used to the Headscarf!"........................... 79
Astrid Wonneberger

Family in the Post-Migrant Society 103
Sabina Stelzig and Katja Weidtmann

Editors and Contributors

About the Editors

PD Dr. Astrid Wonneberger *Department of Social Work, HAW Hamburg*

As a social and cultural anthropologist, Astrid Wonneberger has been a lecturer in the Applied Family Sciences program at the Hamburg University of Applied Sciences and a private lecturer at the Department of Social and Cultural Anthropology at the University of Hamburg since 2012. After many years of ethnographic field work in the Irish diaspora in the USA and in the Dublin Docklands, her academic interests focus on the topics of family, kinship and community, migration, diaspora, ethnicity, and urban anthropology. Since 2018, she has been part of the research team in the BMBF-project POMIKU studying post-migrant family cultures in the Lenzsiedlung in the Hamburg district of Eimsbüttel.

Dr. Sabina Stelzig *Department of Social Work, HAW Hamburg*

After completing her doctorate degree in Sociology on the topic of women's migration, Dr. Sabina Stelzig worked as a research assistant and lecturer in family and migration studies at the University of Hamburg and the Hamburg Institute of International Economics (HWWI). In 2012 she became involved in the development of the Master's program in Applied Family Sciences at the University of Applied Sciences (HAW) Hamburg, where she also teaches Sociology and empirical research methods in the BA Social Work. Since 2018, she has been part of the research team in the BMBF project POMIKU on "post-migrant family cultures".

Prof. Dr. Katja Weidtmann *Department of Social Work, HAW Hamburg*

After her studies in Psychology and Child and Adolescent Psychiatry at the University of Hamburg, Katja Weidtmann worked as a research assistant at the

Medical Faculty and at the Clinic for Child and Adolescent Psychiatry, Psychotherapy and Psychosomatics of the University Medical Center Hamburg-Eppendorf. Here she also received her doctorate with an evaluation study of the special outpatient clinic "Giftedness Center". After working as a school psychologist in Lower Saxony and in Hamburg and in a practice for child and adolescent psychiatry and psychotherapy, she became a research assistant at the University of Applied Sciences (HAW) Hamburg in 2012, helped to establish the Master's program in Applied Family Sciences and has been a professor for Family Psychology and Family Counseling since 2016. She is also the head of the Master's program in Applied Family Sciences and of the research project POMIKU.

Diana Lölsdorf, M.A. *Department of Social Work, HAW Hamburg*

Diana Lölsdorf studied Social Work at the University of Applied Sciences Ostfriesland and Family Sciences at the Hamburg University of Applied Sciences (HAW Hamburg). After many years of leadership in early childhood education, she has been working as a research assistant at the HAW Hamburg in the BMBF research project POMIKU (post-migrant family cultures) since 2018.

Contributors

Silke Hans Institut für Soziologie, Georg-August-Universität Göttingen, Göttingen, Germany

Diana Lölsdorf Department Soziale Arbeit, HAW Hamburg, Hamburg, Germany

Katja Nowacki Fachbereich Angewandte Sozialwissenschaften, Fachhochschule, Dortmund, Germany

Silke Remiorz Fachbereich Angewandte Sozialwissenschaften, Fachhochschule, Dortmund, Germany

Katja Sabisch Gender Studies, Ruhr-Universität, Bochum, Germany

Sabina Stelzig Fakultät W&S, Department Soziale Arbeit, HAW Hamburg, Hamburg, Germany

Katja Weidtmann Department Soziale Arbeit, HAW Hamburg, Hamburg, Germany

Astrid Wonneberger Department Soziale Arbeit, HAW Hamburg, Hamburg, Germany

Introduction: Values and Value Change in the Post-Migrant Society

Astrid Wonneberger, Sabina Stelzig, Diana Lölsdorf and Katja Weidtmann

1 Migration and Societal Change

Immigration to Germany is not a new phenomenon; moreover, its social and cultural consequences have long been discussed and researched. In this context, cultural and social values and norms and their transformation processes play a special role. Cultural pluralization is leading to an increasing diversity in terms of values and norms—which, however, cannot be attributed solely to migration processes—so that today a wider range of values and norms seems to exist than a few decades ago. Some values and norms are changing or even disappearing completely, while others are emerging anew. Such changes are controversially discussed in our society: Which ones are positive, i.e. desired consequences of this value change and which transformations are negatively connotated and thus undesirable? In this context, there is great debate about the best way to secure societal cohesion and to support integration and general participation, two of the major goals in our society.

A. Wonneberger (✉) · S. Stelzig · D. Lölsdorf · K. Weidtmann
Department Soziale Arbeit, HAW Hamburg, Hamburg, Germany
e-mail: astrid.wonneberger@haw-hamburg.de

S. Stelzig
e-mail: sabina.stelzig@haw-hamburg.de

D. Lölsdorf
e-mail: diana.loelsdorf@haw-hamburg.de

K. Weidtmann
e-mail: katja.weidtmann@haw-hamburg.de

© The Author(s), under exclusive license to Springer Fachmedien Wiesbaden GmbH, part of Springer Nature 2024
A. Wonneberger et al. (eds.), *Values and Value Change in the Post-Migrant Society*, https://doi.org/10.1007/978-3-658-45107-3_1

Cultural pluralization can, on the one hand, release potentials and modernization impulses, in terms of transnational relationships, for example, intercultural competencies and cosmopolitan attitudes. On the other hand, pluralization can also increase the risk of a society to drift apart and thus help to enhance a social divide. Values and norms resp. value formation play a central role in this context, as they are a fundamental for integration processes; they fulfill several functions that are crucial for the design of both individual lives and the peaceful coexistence of people, communities, and societies. What basic values and rules should apply for living together in a society? The commitment to rules and values determines a "common denominator", which is to ensure social cohesion. Hradil (2018, p. 29) speaks of values as the "glue of society".[1] The mediation, appropriation, reflection and negotiation of values and norms therefore play a central role for the current and future design of social cohesion, especially in societies that are characterized by migration and cultural diversity.

The topic of "cultural pluralization", briefly outlined here, is one of the focal points of the BMBF funding line "Migration and Societal Change", which has been funding research projects throughout Germany since November 2017 (BMBF 2016, 2020). The present anthology presents results of various projects which have been financed by this funding line. It originated in a workshop focusing on "Values and Cultural Change", coordinated by the University of Applied Sciences Hamburg (HAW Hamburg) in November 2020.

The research questions that arise against the background outlined above are diverse: Which values and associated norms are discussed in our society? Which values are particularly prone to conflicts, particularly in the integration process? Which debates are intensified or exacerbated by a growing cultural diversity? How important are which values? Are there everyday situations and role models in which certain values become particularly relevant?

At a general level, one can also ask which values are affected by change at all and how they change. Can we speak of a loss of values and/or of a growing plurality of values? In which subgroups of our society do which value concepts change? Do values and norms which have been "imported" from other cultures change during the individual integration process? Which shared and long-established values and norms in the host society are affected by change? What adapta-

---

[1] All statements quoted from sources originally published in German were translated by DEEPL and revised by the authors for accuracy.

tion efforts are expected from which members or parts of our society? What kinds of change are necessary if social cohesion is to be ensured in the future?

Finally, the question arises as to how large the differences in cultural and individual values actually are. Where and between which groups are relevant differences noticeable and where are these differences not or hardly present at all? How can these differences and commonalities be explained?

The research contributions included in this volume approach these questions from different perspectives, in various settings and with diverse research designs. Before introducing the projects involved, the concept of a post-migrant society is introduced as a common conceptual framework. In order to unambiguously interpret and present research findings on the topics of "values, norms, attitudes, behavior", to relate the results to each other's findings and to be able to discuss them, more precise definitions of the relevant terms are necessary, as will become clear in the further course of this introduction. After a brief presentation of the research projects, the introductory chapter will conclude with overarching insights deducted from the results of the individual contributions, thus answering the research questions raised above.

2 Conceptual Framework: The Post-Migrant Society

The debate about cultural values and norms and their transformation processes is currently embedded in the discussion about a "post-migrant society" or a "post-migrant perspective". This view of societal transformation processes forms the conceptual framework of the present publication.

The term "post-migration" was first used in 1995 in an edited volume by Baumann and Sunier (Baumann and Sunier 1995; cf. Gaonkar 2021a, p. 14). However, its growing popularity is not attributed to the academic context, but to the founding of the "Post-Migrant Theater", which Shermin Langhoff founded together with colleagues in Berlin in 2008. Since then, the use of the term has not only been popular in cultural work, journalism, and politics, but the term has also found its way into social and cultural sciences, particularly in the German-speaking world (Espahangizi 2016; Foroutan et al. 2018, p. 9; Gaonkar et al. 2021b). Only recently has the term "post-migrant" re-appeared internationally, for instance at conferences within Europe (e.g. The Postmigrant Condition 2018), where it is now also discussed (Römhild 2018, for Switzerland Espahangizi 2016, 2018; see as the latest comprehensive contribution Gaonkar et al. 2021a).

The term "post-migrant society" or "post-migration" denotes a shift in the perspective on migration (Yildiz 2015, p. 19 f.). Similar and analogous to the post-colonial discourse, this term conveys the idea of "retelling the history of migration and radically rethinking the entire field of migration" (Yildiz 2015, p. 21) or "establishing a new understanding of migration" (Yildiz 2015, p. 23). Many authors have taken up and used this term in recent years, including primarily Erol Yildiz and Marc Hill (Yildiz and Hill 2015a; Hill and Yildiz 2018), Foroutan (2016, 2019), Foroutan et al. (2018) and Espahangizi (2016). Central to this change of perspective on migration are the following characteristics and demands:

- Political and societal recognition of being an immigration society and the associated view of migration as a permanent process that significantly contributes to the shaping of society (Foroutan 2016).
- Moving away from a perspective that focuses on people as objects of integration and assimilation, but instead adopts their views and accepts new perceptions of the "in-between". In this context, transnational realities can also be located (Yildiz and Hill 2015b, p. 10 f.; Yildiz 2015, p. 22).
- Moving away from the stereotypical view of migration as a threat to society and a state of emergency, from equating immigration with parallel societies, ghettos, and societal problems (Yildiz and Hill 2015b, p. 10, 23), and from perceiving migrants as deficient, pre-modern, and a threat to democracy (Foroutan et al. 2018, p. 10). Instead, the term "post-migration" should serve to adopt a differentiated view of migration as normality.
- Criticism of labels such as "migrants", "foreigners" or "people with a migratory background" (Yildiz 2015, p. 27) and the demand of breaking up widespread and entrenched dualisms and binary categories: German/foreigners, us/them, western/non-western etc. (Yildiz 2015, p. 21; Foroutan et al. 2018, p. 11).

The concept of post-migration is thus primarily a reaction to predominantly negative assessments and views on migration and includes criticism against and demands on politics, society, and social sciences. Migration research is also criticized in this context, as it has long served and reinforced these rigid and one-sided views in its studies on "guest workers", "foreigners", and integration (Yildiz and Hill 2015, p. 11).

However, this criticism against migration research did not originate with the discourse on post-migration, but dates to the beginning of the 1990s and has long since led to new approaches, such as discussions and studies on transnationalism, diaspora, global networks etc. (for a brief summary see e.g. Haug 2000; Pries 2001). Instead of viewing migration as a unilinear process leading to assimilation, transnationalism and diaspora studies have been focusing on mobility, multiple identities, multilocality, and social networks, using—among other analytical approaches—a transnational concept of culture. However, even these research approaches can only partially meet the demands of the post-migrant perspective. Because—as the cultural and social anthropologist Regina Römhild (2015, 2018) puts it—the focus on transnational lifestyles and identities have created new dualisms which the research had actually intended to break up: on the one hand, the potentially mobile and cross-border networks of migrants, which are thus located on the margins of society, and, on the other hand, those of a locally fixed nation, which forms the center of society (ibid. 2018, p. 70). In addition, many studies could not always live up to their own intentions, as they often retained the old established categories of ethnic affiliation; they often focused on minorities on the margins of society, ethnic interfaces, and multiethnic constellations (Römhild 2015, p. 38).

This indicates the central dilemma of migration research which wants to adopt a critical, post-migrant perspective: On the one hand, migration—also in research—should be recognized as a societal normality. To do this, however, it must be labelled and addressed (Römhild 2015, p. 39). On the one hand, research should adopt the perspectives of people with migration experiences, but on the other hand, these must also be designated and marked as such. On the one hand, labels, and categories such as "foreigners" or "people with a migratory background" determine affiliations and boundaries, transmit stereotypical views, reduce people to certain characteristics, and are accordingly discussed and criticized (Fouroutan et al. 2018, p. 12; Yildiz 2015, p. 27). Categorization also implies the levelling of differences. This can, for example, have the effect that actual relations are obscured when people are classified in such large and heterogeneous categories such as "migrants" or "people with a migratory background", as will also be shown by the results of the research projects involved here. On the other hand, these categorizations are necessary to capture inequalities, e.g. in statistical surveys (Fouroutan et al. 2018, p. 12). Without categories (however they are labelled), migration, migrant experiences, cultural differences etc. cannot be described and studied.

Römhild therefore suggests not to focus research on specific ethnic/cultural groups, but instead to study entire neighborhoods including all social and cultural networks and references that are relevant to the actors. Thus, a complex picture can emerge which is not based on predetermined and often absurd classifications (Römhild 2015, p. 40 f.).

The contributions presented in this volume show that such categories cannot be completely abandoned in research and their use does not fundamentally contradict a post-migrant perspective. We therefore suggest not to avoid categories and labels in general, but to apply them carefully and only when they are necessary to answer scientific questions which can otherwise not be addressed, and in a way which does not further strengthen outdated clichés.

In the project POMIKU, for example, "person with a migratory background" was not used as a category in a survey on family role models; instead "native language" was considered a better and sufficient indicator for cultural differences. In the project JUMEN, this reflective approach led to decision not to designate the cultural backgrounds of the young men studied, as these were not considered relevant for the description of differences. These methodological decisions were based on considerations as to whether differences between people with and without a migration background exist at all and how large (or small) these differences really are. Hans (AFFIN), Remiorz, Nowacki, and Sabisch (JUMEN), Wonneberger (POMIKU), and Stelzig and Weidtmann (POMIKU) reflect this question in their contributions in this volume.

Moreover, it should be a concern of science, politics, and society to counter stereotypical images of migration and of people with a migration background by describing and portraying the realities of people in a differentiated way. Not the abolition of the category "migration" is decisive, because migration will always be part of our society in the future. It would be rather important to revalue or reassess migration, or just view it as a neutral phenomenon. As Andreas Niederberger (2021, p. 98) states, hardly any other research subject in the humanities and social sciences is so determined by values—in the sense of evaluations— and normative judgments as migration. Instead of viewing migration exclusively problem-oriented or only focusing on desired consequences of migration for our society, a reflective and non-judging view, including diverse aspects and perspectives, would be appropriate. Therefore, despite the dilemmas and challenges mentioned above, the term post-migrant is quite suitable for making the required shift in science, politics, and society more visible, or, as Römhild (2018, p. 79) wrote, "to mark the constitutive and creative power of migration in a 'post-migrant' society, which still denies this power."

In summary, this volume understands a "post-migrant society" as a society in which migrant influences are indispensable. Migration is understood as a process that significantly contributes to the shaping of society. The term "post-migrant" also implies the demand that it should be a matter of course for politics and society to understand and acknowledge Germany as a country of immigration, and that migration has long been influencing our society and culture and will continue to do so. In recent years, this view of Germany as a country of immigration has increasingly gained acceptance (cf. e.g. Zick and Krott 2021, p. 4). The announcement of the BMBF funding line (BMBF 2016, 2020), within which this volume was created, also testifies to this. However, this is not happening in our society without any conflicts. Although reported attacks against refugees have been declining since 2016 according to official figures (Deutscher Bundestag 2021), there has also been an increase in racially or "xenophobically" motivated crimes (Bundesinnenministerium 2021, p. 7). Nevertheless, there is a great acceptance in the German population to recognize a variety of cultural lifestyles, identities, and values as normal (Zick and Krott 2021, p. 4–6) and skepticism towards immigration is currently decreasing (Kösemen and Wieland 2022).

This anthology thus aims at moving away from established hegemonic discourses about "parallel societies", from outdated dualisms ("Germans" vs. "foreigners") or views of "native normality and immigrated problems" (Yildiz 2015, p. 22) and instead acknowledging the fact that the interaction of diverse cultural influences occurs in such a complex way that a rigid categorization of people according to certain cultures, backgrounds, and characteristics makes no sense. Accordingly, each contribution has chosen carefully in which contexts which labels and categories are useful and necessary and in which they are not.

3 Terms and Analytical Levels: Values, Norms, Attitudes, Behavior

When dealing with "values", one quickly realizes that the term is related to several other terms, which are often not differentiated (cf. Lang 1994). These include particularly the terms "norms", "attitudes", and "behavior".

All these terms have already been extensively discussed, and it seems almost impossible to come up with definitions that consider all the different disciplinary traditions and perspectives. The definitions of the terms outlined below are therefore to be understood as the lowest common denominator for the contributions in this anthology. In individual cases, the characteristics in the contributions may be formulated somewhat differently or supplemented by further features, as seems appropriate and necessary for the respective study.

Value statements (axiological statements) ascribe evaluations to facts, patterns of action, things etc. Thus, they determine what is "good", "bad" or "neutral" (cf. Lang 1994, p. 171) and therefore "desirable" or not (Kluckhohn 1951; cf. Hradil 2018). There are values that claim to be valid for the entire world (e.g. human rights), other values are culturally shaped and thus not universally valid. *Cultural values* in this volume are values that are shared and passed on by people of a certain society (or parts of a society). Even if this implies a certain level of immutability, cultural values are not rigid, but changeable, just like any other aspect of culture.[2]

Closely linked to values are *norms*. Norms, especially behavioral norms, are concrete prescriptions for social action. They determine how people should behave in certain situations, what they may, should or must do, or what they must not do. Norms prohibit, prescribe, or allow certain behavior. While values can in principle be attributed to anything, normative sentences are more restricted.[3] Values often underlie norms; they are used to justify norms, not vice versa.[4] Norms (e.g. in the form of laws) can in turn serve to protect (basic) values. In this way, values and especially norms provide orientation on how to behave appropriately. They regulate and shape the behavior of individuals and especially interactions and relationships between people, communities and within a society (cf. among others Lang 1994; Zentrum für Globale Fragen 2017).

Although norms are supposed to regulate the *behavior* of people, this does not mean that all people always adhere to the relevant norms. The actual behavior can thus deviate from the norm, at times or permanently. For this reason, the level of behavior must be analytically distinguished from the level of values and the level of norms (cf. Lang 1994).

Intracultural variance characterizes the handling of values, i.e. many individual designs and interpretations are accepted within a society when it comes to interpret and live values and norms. This means that individuals may have different *attitudes* within a cultural value system (which can also result in varying behaviors). In contrast to culturally shared values, attitudes, which also evaluate actions, facts etc., are "exclusively attributed to individuals" (Thome 2019, p. 57). They can therefore also be referred to as *"personal values"* or *"value attitudes"*. These two terms should therefore be used synonymously in this anthology.

---

[2] The concept of culture has also been discussed extensively. In summary, we refer to Beer (2017).

[3] This can be illustrated using a simple example (Lang 1994, p. 172 f.): Earthquakes can be given a value statement (e.g., "it is bad that an earthquake happens"), but not norms—one cannot allow or prohibit earthquakes.

[4] For example, it is forbidden to kill people because human lives are considered valuable. The reversal, because it is forbidden to kill people, human lives are valuable, would make no sense.

Individual attitudes can differ from cultural values, but usually cultural values also shape the attitudes of individuals, because during socialization, people in a specific society (or culture, milieus etc.) learn what is needed to behave appropriately. People are shaped by their cultural values, but this imprint is not static; it can change in life and be adapted to new circumstances, which can also lead to cultural change (cf. Beer 2017, p. 74): When people change their attitudes so that they deviate from the shared patterns of values in a society and if, at the same time, their attitudes coincide with those of many others, the new patterns of shared personal values become cultural values. Individual attitudes and cultural values therefore influence each other: Attitudes can become cultural values when they are shared by many others; cultural values also shape the attitudes of individuals. It is an empirical question where exactly the boundary between cultural, social, i.e. shared values and individual preferences and attitudes lies and how individual attitudes and cultural or collective values mutually influence each other.

The distinction between and the characteristics of the related concepts of values, norms, attitudes, and behaviors outlined above allow several observations which could be significant in the exploration of this topic and were therefore included in the studies presented in this anthology.

The first observation is the *differentiation of the analytical levels* of the four related concepts: It is possible, for example, that there are cases in which no or hardly any differences between cultural values exist, yet the ways how they are transferred to behavioral norms and actions can vary distinctively. Similarly, a conceptual distinction between cultural (shared and widespread) values and individual attitudes can be crucial for the analysis and interpretation of (perceived) cultural differences.

It may also be useful to include the *value context* into the analysis of empirical data. Value systems often seem at first glance to be contradictory, and individual values seem to compete with other values. Sometimes values also limit each other. For example, the value of security (implemented, for example, by surveillance cameras) can contradict the principle (and underlying value) of freedom (cf. Hradil 2018, p. 22 f.). But these contradictions can often be explained if one considers the specific situation or context in which or for which the values apply. The following research questions arise from this observation: Which values are at stake in which situation? Under which conditions do the corresponding norms apply?

Also, the *value hierarchy* can be significant, as not all values in a society are considered equally important and equally binding. Particularly important values are protected accordingly (e.g. by laws), but they are at the same time often rather abstract, which allows a greater range of interpretation how to handle them (cf. Hradil 2018, pp. 21, 30 ff.). The importance of each value depends on individual, situational or cultural factors, which need to be explored empirically in each individual case. What kind of values are important in the case studies analyzed in this volume? Does the consensus regarding individual attitudes depend on the ascribed importance of the cultural values?

And last but not least: What role do societal discourses on migration play in the perception of values and value change in our society? At this point, the abovementioned reflections on the post-migrant perspective will prove helpful.

4 Involved Projects and Contributions

In total, 23 (joint) projects were funded between 2017 and 2022 in the BMBF funding line "Migration and Societal Change" (BMBF 2016, 2020), three of which present parts of their results in this anthology in four chapters.[5]

The project "Affective and Cultural Dimensions of Integration as a Result of Displacement and Immigration" (AFFIN) is an interdisciplinary research association of sociologists, psychologists, and medical professionals from the field of cross-cultural psychiatry. Located at the Free University of Berlin, the Charité—Universitätsmedizin Berlin, the German Institute for Economic Research (DIW Berlin) and the Georg-August-University Göttingen, the research project focuses on immigration to Germany caused by displacement and migration and its challenges for social coexistence in contemporary society. The aim of the project is to analyze aspects of integration that have only been marginally studied from an interdisciplinary perspective in order to understand societal change through immigration and, finally, to develop action proposals for societal decision-makers. In particular, the role of values, feelings and emotions, aspects of belonging, the sensation of foreignness and familiarity, and affective well-being are analyzed, both on the part of migrants and refugees and on the part of the native population (FU Berlin 2021).

In her contribution "Traditional Values—Lack of Integration? Gender Role Orientations as Explanatory Factors for the Structural Integration of Refugee

---

[5] In the original German version of this anthology there are seven contributions and four projects (in addition to those listed here: Tongue). Due to legal restrictions, not all contributions can be published as translations in this volume. Missing are Fuchs and von Scheve (2023); Bührig and Mittag (2023); and Fischer, Kohlen, and Könninger (2023).

Women in Germany" Silke Hans (AFFIN) looks for explanations for the observation that immigrant women and especially mothers fare worse in many areas of structural integration compared to immigrant men or fathers, especially in terms of their positioning in the labor market. This applies to both asylum seekers and migrants who have come to Germany for other reasons. Based on the data from the IAB-BAMF-SOEP survey, a representative longitudinal study on refugees in Germany, and the World Values Survey, Hans investigates whether, in addition to a lack of human capital and the presence of children, traditional orientations regarding the role of women and men also influence the structural integration of refugee women in Germany. She concludes that traditional gender role orientations among refugee women—unlike men—actually lead to lower investments in human capital, i.e., they have less knowledge of German, have lower employment intentions and a lower employment rate.

The project "Attitudes of Young Men with and without Migration History to Gender and LGBTI in a Changing, Diverse Society" (JUMEN), which is based at the Dortmund University of Applied Sciences and the Ruhr University Bochum, also deals with values and norms regarding gender and gender roles. The joint project investigates how boys and men aged between 14 and 27 with and without a migration history experience their own gender roles and what attitudes they have towards girls and women, homosexuality, and gender diversity (trans- and intersexuality). The project responds to the current societal debate, which, at the latest since the assaults on women on New Year's Eve 2015/16, attributes a traditional and/or misogynistic attitude to young Muslim men with a refugee and migration background. The aim is to identify needs for action regarding values and norms in order to transfer these into prevention strategies against sexual violence and discrimination (FH Dortmund 2021).

The chapter "Attitudes and Value Orientation of Young Men towards Gender and Equality in Germany" presents results from the project JUMEN. Based on 62 qualitative interviews conducted with young men with and without a migration history about their attitudes towards gender relations, Silke Remiorz, Katja Nowacki, and Katja Sabisch conclude that all interviewees express a generally positive attitude towards the equality of women and men and show openness to change regarding gender roles. However, when asked specifically about their own potential partnership, a rather traditional attitude of all respondents, regardless of their background, becomes apparent. This indicates a preservation of values. The authors' analysis shows that a change in traditional gender relations requires a discussion in the entire society which goes beyond widespread stereotypes and prejudices.

The project "Post-Migrant Family Cultures" (POMIKU) is represented in this volume with two contributions. Based on mixed-method research in the large housing estate Lenzsiedlung in Hamburg-Eimsbüttel, the joint project of the University of Applied Sciences Hamburg (HAW Hamburg), the University of Hamburg and Lenzsiedlung e. V. investigates how culturally different forms of family life affect social cohesion and communal living in the neighborhood. Norms and values in relation to family and everyday life in the large housing estate is one of the key topics in this research, but the role of languages in the process of arrival and communal living in the neighborhood is also addressed (HAW Hamburg 2021; POMIKU 2021).

Dealing with diversity and cultural differences is part of everyday life for the nearly 3,000 residents of the Lenzsiedlung. More than 70% of the inhabitants have a migratory background and come from over 60 countries. Based on exemplary observations of situations of conflict and reflective statements from residents, Astrid Wonneberger analyzes residents' attitudes towards the perception of cultural differences. Her contribution "'One has gotten used to the headscarf!' On dealing with cultural differences in a Hamburg housing estate" shows that attitudes towards cultural differences are shaped by attitudes towards migration in general and by personal values and norms regarding family (especially in relation to gender relations, parenting and raising children) and religion (especially in relation to Islam). The results demonstrate that individual attitudes are influenced by living in a culturally diverse housing estate, particularly if the residents get in direct contact with each other. In the cases studied, a growing reflection of residents' attitudes can be observed, which can lead to an increasing acceptance of cultural diversity. However, the data also reveal limits of tolerance, particularly if fundamental values are perceived as threatened. Widespread stereotypes and culturalized views of behavior also have an impact on these processes.

Sabina Stelzig and Katja Weidtmann use a different approach in their contribution "Family role models in post-migrant society. Attitudes of and about families in a large housing estate". On the one hand, their contribution deals with the diversity of normative role models among the residents of the neighborhood, on the other hand it takes a close look at factors influencing personal attitudes towards "how a family should be". Thus, the authors provide an alternative perspective to a problem-oriented view of families in large housing estates which often characterize popular images in politics and multi-media. These images often include generalized ideas of people living in "incomplete" or "broken" families, of parents who show (too) little interest in their (too many) children and do not sufficiently fulfill their care and education duties. Often, this also includes reports of children and adolescents with problems in school and educational deficits due to weak socio-economic status or migration background. The diversity of family life and family forms is as large as the potential problems resulting from this, but resources in "high-rise settlements" can also be identified. Both personal attitudes and perceptions of "normal", "good" or "right" families popular in the social environment play a major role in understanding family practices in the housing estate studied, as everywhere in society. The contribution reveals value conceptions which serve as guidelines for family life in a post-migrant society by examining questions of belonging to and functions of family, attitudes in relation to the education of children and expectations of (gender) roles in the family.

5 Shared Outcomes and Insights

One initial question of this anthology addresses which values are particularly discussed in our society. Not all values seem to provide equally explosive material for societal conflicts in the context of immigration and integration processes. Rather, it appears that those values that are generally changing through social and cultural transformation processes in our society, even independently of immigration, are particularly in the focus of debates. Especially spheres that have been long fought over, and conceptions of values that apparently cannot yet be fully met, seem to be particularly emotionally charged, as people might be afraid that they could be lost again. Such fears are probably particularly widespread, as this change of values and norms could go in a "wrong", because "backward", direction (cf. Lingen-Ali and Mecheril 2020). These worries and debates seem to gain new relevance be intensified due to growing cultural diversity, and immigration quickly comes under suspicion of being the main cause of this dynamic.

These and other societal discourses can also be found in the research topics involved in this anthology, which mainly deal with questions that touch on basic values, such as family, gender, and gender roles, education, religion, security, and democracy. Numerous other studies are also available on all these topics (e.g. Barz et al. 2015; Zentrum für globale Fragen 2017; Freise and Khorchide 2014; BMFSFJ 2010; Rodenstock and Sevsay-Tegethoff 2018; BAMF 2016 and many others). In some cases, it is also noticeable that there appears to be a hierarchy of values depending on the situation: for example, the equality of men and women and security are considered more important in concrete encounters than religious freedom, as the criticism of veils and burkas by residents in the project POMIKU illustrates.

The actors in the studies presented in this volume are different groups in various settings: On the one hand, the views of those are examined who are considered "foreign" or "newcomers" and who are held responsible for the perceived "German" value change. Those are particularly people who have only recently come to Germany as refugees and asylum seekers with the waves of immigration to Europe in 2015 and 2016. These groups are mainly looked at by the projects AFFIN and JUMEN.

On the other hand, the focus also lies on those who have been living in Germany for a long time, the "locals", who are concerned about a loss of values. Their attitudes are studied by the project POMIKU, which looks at the relationships between people of different cultural backgrounds in a housing estate and examines the negotiation processes of values in specific situations.

Some overall outcomes can be generated by comparing the results of the participating projects. They are introduced here in the form of two theses,[6] before the results of the individual studies will be presented. At this point, it should be noted again that these overall insights are based on the post-migrant debate which criticizes oversimplifying and mostly negative views on migration, which are so popular in our society. The overall findings presented here are intended to help reflect such entrenched views and, in the best case, to break them up.

Thesis 1: Differences in values and attitudes between people of different cultural origins are not as large as often assumed

The studies presented here reinforce the knowledge already generated in many other studies that attitudes towards many basic values do not differ as much as often assumed in various cultural groups (cf. e.g. Kohlbacher et al. 2017; Kohlbacher 2017; Baier and Böhm 2018; Brücker et al. 2016a, b; Fuchs et al. 2020; BMFSFJ 2010, p. 16; Uslucan 2013a, p. 238 f., b; IfD Allensbach 2020; Werte-Index 2020; Encyclopedia of Wertvorstellungen 2020; Klinkhammer and Neumaier 2020; Zentrum für globale Frage 2017, p. 25, 63), even though differences can certainly be identified depending on the specific value perception and within the group of immigrants (Buber-Ennser et al. 2016).

As the project JUMEN shows, young men of various cultural backgrounds have a quite similar positive attitude towards the equality of women and men, but at the same time prefer a similar traditional family image for their own partnership—regardless of their descent. The surveys thus do not confirm the widespread concern that migrated young men have a particularly backward image of women and an anti-emancipatory attitude due to their cultural or religious origin. Instead, the

---

[6] In the German version, three theses are presented and discussed. Due to the missing three contributions the third thesis cannot be mentioned and elaborated here.

article shows that the discussion about gender and equality should be less focused on immigration, immigrants, and refugees, but requires a debate which includes the entire German society.

The project POMIKU concludes that family role models of people with a non-German native language are only more conservative than those of German native speakers in terms of a few, specific aspects. No significant differences were found between Turkish and German native speakers. Family life in the housing estate studied is extremely diverse, but at the same time the ideas of a "good" family life are not as different as one might expect from residents who originate from over 60 countries. However, differences between Turkish and German native speakers do occur with regards to functions of the family. This becomes clear, for example, when interviewees are asked about the importance of children. In addition to explanations that focus on a generally stronger role of family in families of Turkish descent, further explanatory approaches are offered. One reason could be that parents who were born in Turkey and only later immigrated to Germany could hardly have gained the experience that they can rely on state support in old age, unlike parents who were born in Germany. In addition, Turkish native speakers see the parents as more responsible for the education and educational success of their children than German native speakers, which could be explained from the same context.

Widespread perceptions and concerns that the increased immigration from predominantly non-Western countries over the past years could affect democracy, gender equality, and the principles of a liberal and secular state—which the post-migrant approach also criticizes—can barely or not be supported by the available data.

Several approaches help to explain why the public perception is often so distorted:

The first approach addresses the problem of stereotyping. Several of the contributions presented show that differences may be overemphasized, and similarities overlooked due to long-existing mutual stereotypical images. As the project POMIKU demonstrates, for instance, the attitudes of some residents towards housing estates have long been shaped by stereotypical views on migration, and only after they moved in and made experiences that differed from their original view, they re-evaluated their perception. Personal experience and direct contacts seem to trigger a change in attitude towards people with a migratory background and towards housing estates, and this enables a more differentiated view and reflection of one's own attitudes. The data also provide evidence of common stereotypical notions of Islam, which is associated with gender hierarchies, backwardness, and potential danger. This issue is also addressed by JUMEN. The project AFFIN shows that perceived differences in gender role orientations which are dominated by rejecting attitudes, especially among relevant gatekeepers—e.g. teachers, HR managers, public servants—in the German population, make access to structural integration for immigrants more difficult, especially for women. All these cases illustrate that stereotypical attributions can hinder integration by emphasizing the extent of differences and thus influencing people's attitudes towards people with a migratory background, which in turn can lead to discriminatory behavior.

The problem of stereotyping is closely linked to the phenomenon of culturalization, i.e., attributions based on (assumed) cultural differences, while in fact individual attitudes are in effect. Uslucan (2013a, p. 237) has already pointed out this problem. Values are shared and passed on as part of culture, but not all individual value statements are necessarily also culturally shared views. Instead, they can be based on individual attitudes that—if at all—only reflect a part of the culturally shared values. An excessive focus on culture as a decisive factor, with might help to explain perceived differences, often falls short. It stands for a concept of culture that sees individuals as determined by culture and oversees their ability to develop their personality and adapt opinions to new situations. In the worst case, such stereotypical evaluations and attributions can even lead to classify a personal discrepancy as a form of "cultural conflict" (cf. e.g. Uslucan 2013b, p. 253; Lingen-Ali and Mecheril 2020). The project POMIKU, for example, observed situations which point to culturalized views, particularly in terms of how to raise children. Stereotypical attributions and culturalization can distort perceptions of existing differences.

The second approach distinguishes between the analytical levels of cultural values, norms, individual attitudes, and actual behavior. Apparently, in certain situations, conflicts, or debates, it is not so much about values, but rather about the implementation of these into concrete behavioral norms, the evaluation of these norms, or actual behavior. This may also depend on the actual context. This was also pointed out by the BMFSFJ 2010: The family and its care function, for example, represent an important value for all (cultural and social) groupings. However, the way family is designed and acted out, e.g. with regards to transfer services or responsibility, can be very different.

Examples can also be found in the cases presented in this volume: As said before, the basic values of our society are shared and accepted by the vast majority, regardless of their migratory or cultural background. In the project POMIKU, for example, it becomes clear that family is a widespread and shared basic value and children are an asset across cultures. However, the ideas about the concrete behavioral *norms*, what a family should be like and what not, what makes a "good" family, how children should be raised and what rights and duties they have etc., not only differ individually, but can also be shaped by cultural belief systems. Corresponding findings and observations are therefore to be presented, interpreted, and discussed according to the corresponding analytical level.

As a third consideration, it should be mentioned here that studies usually explore attitudes and values at a specific point in time and in the context of specific situations, not as a changing process. For example, if you ask people who have just migrated to Germany, their answers may be shaped by their current status within the immigration process. Depending on the context and experience in the host country, these attitudes and expectations can adapt in one direction or another or remain stable.

Thesis 2: Differences concerning values and attitudes do not only run along ethnic/national/cultural boundaries.

The boundaries by which differences in values and attitudes are determined do not always run along ethnic, national or cultural boundaries. In many cases, the shaping of values and attitudes it rather influenced by characteristics that are not based on migration experiences.

The project JUMEN, for instance, concludes that culture or a cultural imprint does not play as big a role in the shaping of individual attitudes as is often assumed in societal discourses. The identified differences rather run "across" national or cultural backgrounds, so that other significant influencing factors are to be assumed. Above all, the specific family situation in which the respondents were socialized seems to play a decisive role, regardless of the migratory background: The interview partners, regardless of which cultural background, who grew up in traditional nuclear families dominated by traditional gender images in relation to childcare and household tasks, also maintain a rather traditional attitude regarding gender relations, and this also has an impact on how family life is shaped and lived.

The project AFFIN also finds that many differences in attitudes do not primarily run along cultural boundaries but can also be found within the native "German" population: As Hans shows in her contribution, traditional gender role attitudes have similar effects on the integration into the labor market for people without a migratory background; however, in those cases nobody talks about a lack of or insufficient integration. Moreover, the category "migratory background" proves to be too heterogeneous to be a suitable category to present the differentiated findings. Instead, from the author's point of view, it is advisable to distinguish between the exact places of origin, as this might point to existing cultural differences. Finally, the level of education is emphasized as an important correlating characteristic.

In addition to linguistic and cultural backgrounds, which do play a role in the evaluation of individual characteristics, the project POMIKU identifies particularly the factors age, family form and gender which determine differences in attitudes towards family role models.

These findings also coincide with other studies, including the Sinus-Milieu study, which also depicts the great diversity of migrant lifestyles and concludes that cultural backgrounds hardly determine basic orientations and value attitudes (Flaig and Schleer 2018, p. 116).

All these explanatory approaches demonstrate that culture can indeed play a role in terms of values and attitudes. However, boundaries and categorizations should be made carefully and not be based on cultural differences only, as in many cases other factors seem to be equally important to explain observed differences.

6 Conclusion

Several ideas can be derived from all these findings regarding a post-migrant perspective. On the one hand, it becomes clear that there is no way around perceiving Germany as a country of immigration. Migration is a permanent process that will continue to shape our society in the future. The process of societal change is diverse, multilinear and complex, all members and actors of society (science, politics, support systems etc.) are both actively and passively involved in this change: In the context of integration, "newcomers" adapt to the new (cultural) environment and at the same time influence the "locals", directly (in contact situations) or indirectly (e.g. through reflections). Some situations of conflict might require a debate about prevailing value standards and corresponding norms. Crucial for adopting a post-migrant perspective is the ongoing process of reflection and the exploration of value and norm boundaries, which increasingly blurs the boundaries between "local" and "immigrated".

The results of the research projects presented in this volume underline the insight that a differentiated view of migration is necessary to analyze diversity, differences, but also conflicts—in this case about values, norms, and behavior—and to be able to deal with them. As the results of the projects AFFIN, JUMEN and POMIKU show, the focus on migration alone is not sufficient to describe and explain existing differences in individual attitudes: In addition to the specific cultural background, it is primarily culture-independent variables that seem to play a role in the formation of values and therefore need to be considered. If, however, migration is focused on too much or too strongly, there is a risk of overemphasizing the importance of culture and migration in this context. This implies a threat of stigmatization of certain groups solely because of their migratory background or assumed cultural differences, as particularly JUMEN illustrates for young Muslim men.

The results presented in this anthology can certainly provide arguments for the existence of differences that may contain a potential to cause societal conflicts and thus hinder the integration of immigrants and their descendants. However, the data also show that such differences, especially in relation to attitudes towards basic values, are apparently less dominant than assumed by certain parts of the population and often overemphasized by the media. None of the studies provides evidence that democratic values are threatened, and a general loss of values is not observable, especially not in relation to basic values. Rather, there seems to be a pluralization of values, norms, and attitudes. Even if the research projects provide findings that can be assessed as threats to democracy or equality, these are not exclusively or clearly located along cultural or national boundaries, and it makes no sense to tie them to migration only. Therefore, a differentiated view is needed to analyze existing diversity, differences, but also conflicts—in this case about values, norms, and behavior—and to develop ideas how to deal with them. This is the approach that was chosen by the research projects presented here. They show that the discussion about values and value change is less a question of immigration or cultural differences, but it is rather embedded in larger societal debates in Germany and should be led accordingly.

References

BAMF. 2016. Wertebildung in der Einwanderungsgesellschaft. Dokumentation der gemeinsamen Tagung des Bundesamtes für Migration und Flüchtlinge und der Bertelsmann Stiftung, Berlin, 10.11.2016. https://www.bertelsmann-stiftung.de/fileadmin/files/Projekte/Wertebildung/Tagungsdokumentation_Wertebildung-in-der-Einwanderungsgesellschaft_final.pdf. Accessed: 15 Dec 2021.

Baier, Andrea, and Axel Böhm. 2018. Mehr Gemeinsamkeiten als Unterschiede? Eine vergleichende Analyse politischer Einstellungen von Personen mit und ohne Fluchterfahrung in Deutschland. Institut für Demokratie und Zivilgesellschaft (IDZ)—Thüringer Dokumentations- und Forschungsstelle gegen Menschenfeindlichkeit (Ed.), *Wissen schafft Demokratie 3/2018 – Gesellschaftlicher Zusammenhalt*, 38–49. Jena: Institut für Demokratie und Zivilgesellschaft (IDZ). https://doi.org/10.19222/201803/04. Accessed: 14 Dec 2021.

Barz, Heiner, Katrin Barth, Meral Cerci-Thoms, Zeynep Dereköy, Mareike Först, Thi Thao Le, and Igor Mitchnik. 2015. Große Vielfalt, weniger Chancen. Eine Studie über die Bildungserfahrungen und Bildungsziele von Menschen mit Migrationshintergrund in

Deutschland. Stiftung Mercator und Vodafone Stiftung Deutschland, Essen, Düsseldorf. https://www.stiftung-mercator.de/media/downloads/3_Publikationen/Barz_Heiner_et_al_Grosse_Vielfalt_weniger_Chancen_Abschlusspublikation.pdf. Accessed: 29 Jun 2021.

Baumann, Gerd, and Thijl Sunier, eds. 1995. *Post-Migration Ethnicity. De-Essentializing Cohesion, Commitments, Comparisons.* Amsterdam: Het Spinhuis.

Beer, Bettina. 2017. Kultur und Ethnizität. In *Ethnologie. Einführung in die Erforschung kultureller Vielfalt.* Eds. Bettina Beer, Hans Fischer, and Julia Pauli, 71–88. 9th ed., Berlin: Reimer.

BMBF. 2016. Bekanntmachung: Richtlinie zur Förderung der Maßnahme „Migration und gesellschaftlicher Wandel" im Rahmen des Forschungsrahmenprogramms „Geistes-, Kultur- und Sozialwissenschaften". Bundesanzeiger vom 15.11.2016. https://www.bmbf.de/foerderungen/bekanntmachung-1272.html. Accessed: 29 Jun 2021.

BMBF. 2020. Migration und gesellschaftlicher Wandel – Förderlinie des Bundesministeriums für Bildung und Forschung. Edited by DLR Projektträger, Bonn, Dec. 2020. https://www.geistes-und-sozialwissenschaften-bmbf.de/files/Foerderlinie_Migration_gesellschaftlicher_Wandel.pdf. Accessed: 29 Jun 2021.

BMFSFJ. 2010. Ehe, Familie, Werte – Migrantinnen und Migranten in Deutschland. Monitor Familienforschung. Beiträge aus Forschung, Statistik und Familienpolitik, Issue 24. https://www.bmfsfj.de/newsletter/bmfsfj/themen/familie/76214?view=DEFAULT. Accessed: 24 Jun 2021.

Brücker, Herbert, Nina Rother, Jürgen Schupp, Christian Babka von Gostomski, Axel Böhm, Tanja Fendel, Martin Friedrich, Marco Giesselmann, Yuliya Kosyakova, Martin Kroh, Elisabeth Liebau, David Richter, Agnese Romiti, Diana Schacht, Jana A. Scheible, Paul Schmelzer, Manuel Siegert, Steffen Sirries, Parvati Trübswetter, and Ehsan Vallizad. 2016a. Flucht, Ankunft in Deutschland und erste Schritte der Integration. *DIW Wochenbericht* 46: 1103–1119.https://www.diw.de/documents/publikationen/73/diw_01.c.546854.de/16-46-4.pdf. Accessed: 5 Oct 2021.

Brücker, Herbert, Astrid Kunert, Ulrike Mangold, Barbara Kalusche, Manuel Siegert, and Jürgen Schupp. 2016b. Geflüchtete Menschen in Deutschland – eine qualitative Befragung. *SOEP Survey Papers 313:* Series C. Berlin: DIW/SOEP. https://www.diw.de/documents/publikationen/73/diw_01.c.570912.de/diw_ssp0313.pdf. Accessed: 5 Oct 2021.

Buber-Ennser, Isabella, Judith Kohlenberger, Bernhard Rengs, Zakarya Al Zalak, Anne Goujon, Erich Striessnig, Michaela Potančoková, Richard Gisser, Maria Testa, and Wolfgang Lutz. 2016. Human capital, values, and attitudes of persons seeking refuge in Austria in 2015. *PLoS one* 11(9). https://doi.org/10.1371/journal.pone.0163481

Bührig, Kristin, und Romy Mittag (2023) Werte und Bewertungsverfahren von Jugendlichen im postmigrantischen Kontext. Exemplarische Analyse zum Positionieren im Interview. In *Werte und Wertewandel in der postmigrantischen Gesellschaft.* Eds. Astrid Wonneberger, Sabina Stelzig, Katja Weidtmann, and Diana Lölsdorf, 187–211. Wiesbaden: Springer.

Bundesinnenministerium. 2021. Politisch motivierte Kriminalität im Jahr 2020. Bundesweite Fallzahlen. https://www.bmi.bund.de/SharedDocs/downloads/DE/veroeffentlichungen/2021/05/pmk-2020-bundesweite-fallzahlen.pdf?__blob=publicationFile&v=4. Accessed: 21 Mar 2022.

Deutscher Bundestag. 2021. Proteste gegen und Übergriffe auf Flüchtlingsunterkünfte im ersten/zweiten/dritten/vierten Quartal 2021. https://dserver.bundestag.de/btd/20/001/2000119.pdf. Accessed: 21 Mar 2022.

Enzyklopädie der Wertvorstellungen. 2020. Ranking der Werte (January 2014-March 2020). https://www.wertesysteme.de/werte-ranking/. Accessed: 24 Jun 2021.

Espahangizi, Kijan. 2016. Das Postmigrantische ist kein Kind der Akademie. Geschichte der Gegenwart. https://geschichtedergegenwart.ch/das-postmigrantische-kein-kind-der-akademie/. Accessed: 19 Aug 2021.

Espahangizi, Kijan. 2018. Ab wann sind Gesellschaften postmigrantisch? In *Postmigrantische Perspektiven. Ordnungssysteme, Repräsentationen, Kritik*. eds. Naika Foroutan, Juliane Karakayali, and Riem Spielhaus, 35–55. Bonn: Bundeszentrale für politische Bildung.

Fischer, Nils, Helen Kohlen, and Sabine Könninger (2023) Übersetzung in deutschen Krankenhäusern. Ein grundlegendes und ethisches Problem. In *Werte und Wertewandel in der postmigrantischen Gesellschaft*. eds. Astrid Wonneberger, Sabina Stelzig, Katja Weidtmann, and Diana Lölsdorf, 213–237. Wiesbaden: Springer

Flaig, Berthold Bodo, and Christoph Schleer. 2018. Migrantische Lebenswelten in Deutschland. Update des Modells der Sinus-Migrantenmilieus. In *Praxis der Sinus-Milieus. Gegenwart und Zukunft eines modernen Gesellschafts- und Zielgruppenmodells*. Eds. Bertram Barth, Berthold Bodo Flaig, Norbert Schäuble, and Manfred Tautscher, 113–123. Wiesbaden: Springer VS.

Foroutan, Naika. 2016. Postmigrantische Gesellschaft. In *Einwanderungsgesellschaft Deutschland*, ed. Heinz-Ulrich. Brinkmann and Martina Sauer, 227–254. Wiesbaden: Springer.

Foroutan, Naika. 2019. *Die postmigrantische Gesellschaft. Ein Versprechen der pluralen Demokratie*. Bielefeld: transcript.

Foroutan, Naika, Juliane Karakayali, and Riem Spielhaus, eds. 2018. *Postmigrantische Perspektiven. Ordnungssysteme, Repräsentationen, Kritik*. Bonn: Bundeszentrale für politische Bildung.

Foroutan, Naika, Juliane Karakayali, and Riem Spielhaus. 2018. Einleitung: Kritische Wissensproduktion zur postmigrantischen Gesellschaft. In *Postmigrantische Perspektiven. Ordnungssysteme, Repräsentationen, Kritik*. Eds. Naika Foroutan, Juliane Karakayali, and Riem Spielhaus, 9–16. Bonn: Bundeszentrale für politische Bildung.

Freise, Josef, and Mouhanad Khorchide, eds. 2014. *Wertedialog der Religionen: Überlegungen und Erfahrungen zu Bildung, Seelsorge, Sozialer Arbeit und Wissenschaft*. Freiburg: Herder Verlag.

FH Dortmund. 2021. JUMEN. Einstellungen junger Männer mit und ohne Zuwanderungsgeschichte zu Gender und LSBTI in einer sich wandelnden, vielfältigen Gesellschaft. https://www.fh-dortmund.de/projekte/jumen.php. Accessed: 29 Jun 2021.

FU Berlin. 2021. Affektive und kulturelle Dimensionen von Integration in Folge von Flucht und Zuwanderung (AFFIN). https://www.polsoz.fu-berlin.de/soziologie/v/affin/index.html Accessed: 29 Jun 2021.

Fuchs, Lukas M., Yu Fan, and Christian von Scheve. 2020. Value Differences between Refugees and German Citizens: Insights from a Representative Survey International Migration https://doi.org/10.1111/imig.12795

Fuchs, Lukas M., and Christian von Scheve. 2023. Werthaltungen Geflüchteter und einheimischer Bevölkerung in Deutschland. In *Werte und Wertewandel in der postmigrantischen Gesellschaft*, ed. Astrid Wonneberger, Sabina Stelzig, Katja Weidtmann, and Diana Lölsdorf, 33–58. Wiesbaden: Springer.

Gaonkar, Anna Meera, Astrid Sophie Øst Hansen, Hans Christian Post, and Moritz Schramm, eds. 2021a. *Postmigration. Art, Culture, and Politics in Contemporary Europe*. Bielefeld: transcript.

Gaonkar, Anna Meera, Astrid Sophie Øst Hansen, Hans Christian Post, and Moritz Schramm. 2021b. Introduction. In *Postmigration. Art, Culture, and Politics in Contemporary Europe*. eds. Anna Meera Gaonkar, Astrid Sophie Øst Hansen, Hans Christian Post und Moritz Schramm, 12–42. Bielefeld: transcript.

HAW Hamburg. 2021. POMIKU. Postmigrantische Familienkulturen. https://www.haw-hamburg.de/forschung/projekte-a-z/forschungsprojekte-detail/project/project/show/pomiku/. Accessed: 29 Jun 2021.

Haug, Sonja. 2000. Klassische und neuere Theorien der Migration. Arbeitspapiere – Mannheimer Zentrum für Europäische Sozialforschung, No. 30. http://www.mzes.uni-mannheim.de/publications/wp/wp-30.pdf. Accessed: 3 Jan 2022.

Hill, Marc, and Erol Yildiz, eds. 2018. *Postmigrantische Visionen. Erfahrungen, Ideen, Reflexionen*. Bielefeld: transcript.

Hradil, Stefan. 2018. Der Wert von Werten: Wozu sind sie gut und wie entstehen sie? In *Werte – und was sie uns wert sind. Eine interdisziplinäre Anthologie*. Eds. Randolf Rodenstock and Nese Sevsay-Tegethoff, 19–36. Munich: RHI-Book, https://www.romanherzoginstitut.de/publikationen/detail/werte-und-was-sie-uns-wert-sind.html. Accessed: 29 Jun 2021.

IfD Allensbach. 2020. Allensbacher Markt- und Werbeträger-Analyse - AWA 2020. Statista 2021. https://de.statista.com/statistik/daten/studie/170820/umfrage/als-besonders-wichtig-erachtete-aspekte-im-leben/. Accessed: June 24, 2021.

Klinkhammer, Gritt, und Anna Neumaier. 2020. *Religiöse Pluralitäten. Umbrüche in der Wahrnehmung religiöser Vielfalt in Deutschland*. Bielefeld: transcript.

Kluckhohn, Clyde. 1951. Values and Value-Orientation in the Theory of Action. An Exploration in Definition and Classification. In *Toward a General Theory of Action*. Eds. Talcott Parsons und Edward A. Shils, 388–433. Cambridge: Harvard University Press.

Kohlbacher, Josef, Gabriele Rasuly-Paleczek, Andreas Hackl, and Sabine Bauer. 2017. *Wertehaltungen und Erwartungen von Asylberechtigten und subsidiär Schutzberechtigten in Österreich*. Österreichische Akademie der Wissenschaften.

Kohlbacher, Josef. 2017. Ein Überblick. Endbericht. Wertehaltungen und Erwartungen von Flüchtlingen in Österreich. 7–51. https://www.bmeia.gv.at/fileadmin/user_upload/Zentrale/Integration/Studien/Studie_Wertehaltungen_und_Erwartungen.pdf. Accessed: 14 Dec 2021.

Kösemen, Orkan, and Ulrike Wieland. 2022. *Willkommenskultur zwischen Stabilität und Aufbruch*. Gütersloh: Bertelsmann Stiftung. https://www.bertelsmann-stiftung.de/en/publications/publication/did/willkommenskultur-zwischen-stabilitaet-und-aufbruch-all. Accessed: 15 Mar 2022.

Lang, Hartmut. 1994. Wissenschaftstheorie für die ethnologische Praxis. 2nd completely revised and expanded edition, Berlin: Reimer.

Lingen-Ali, Ulrike, and Paul Mecheril, eds. 2020. *Geschlechterdiskurse in der Migrationsgesellschaft*. Bielefeld: transcript.

Niederberger, Andreas. 2021. Migrationsethik in der Krise. Einige grundlegende philosophische Überlegungen. *Journal for Migration Research – Journal of Migration Research* 1 (1): 97–123. https://doi.org/10.48439/zmf.v1i1.99. Accessed: 15 Mar 2022.

POMIKU – postmigrantische Familienkulturen. 2021. Joint project page. https://www.familienkulturen.de/. Accessed: 29 Jun 2021.

Pries, Ludger. 2001. *Internationale Migration*. Bielefeld: transcript.

Rodenstock, Randolf, and Nese Sevsay-Tegethoff, eds. 2018. Werte – und was sie uns wert sind. Eine interdisziplinäre Anthologie. Munich: RHI-Book. https://www.romanherzoginstitut.de/publikationen/detail/werte-und-was-sie-uns-wert-sind.html. Accessed: 29 Jun 2021.

Römhild, Regina. 2015. Jenseits ethnischer Grenzen. Für eine postmigrantische Kultur- und Gesellschaftsforschung. In *Nach der Migration. Postmigrantische Perspektiven jenseits der Parallelgesellschaft*. Eds. Erol Yildiz and Marc Hill, 37–48. Bielefeld: transcript.

Römhild, Regina. 2018. Europa postmigrantisch: Entdeckungen jenseits ethnischer, nationaler und kolonialer Grenzen. In *Postmigrantische Perspektiven. Ordnungssysteme, Repräsentationen, Kritik*. Eds. Naika Foroutan, Juliane Karakayali, and Riem Spielhaus, 69–82. Bonn: Bundeszentrale für politische Bildung.

The Postmigrant Condition: Art, Culture and Politics in Contemporary Europe. Conference, 22–23 November 2018, University of Southern Denmark, Odense. https://networks.h-net.org/node/73374/announcements/1975873/%E2%80%9C-postmigrant-condition-art-culture-and-politics-contemporary. Accessed: 24 Aug 2021.

Thome, Helmut. 2019. Werte und Wertebildung aus soziologischer Sicht. In *Werte und Wertebildung aus interdisziplinärer Perspektive*, ed. Roland Verwiebe, 47–77. Wiesbaden: Springer VS.

Uslucan, Haci Halil. 2013a. Lebenswelten und Werte von Migrantinnen. In *Dabeisein und Dazugehören. Integration in Deutschland*. Eds. Heinz Ulrich Brinkmann and Haci Halil Uslucan, 227–248. Wiesbaden: Springer VS.

Uslucan, Haci Halil. 2013b. Vom Wert der Werte in der Lebensführung: Andere Kulturen – andere Werte? In *Werte und Wertebildung in Familien, Bildungsinstitutionen, Kooperationen. Beiträge aus Theorie und Praxis*. Ed. DRK, 247–261. Berlin: https://www.bmfsfj.de/resource/blob/114088/3f1510ae813dbff3b1fb4d474095c125/werte-und-wertebildung-in-familien-bildungsinstitutionen-kooperationen-beitraege-aus-theorie-und-praxis-buch-data.pdf. Accessed: August 16, 2021.

Werte-Index. 2020. *Edited by Peter Wippermann and Jens Krüger*. Frankfurt/M.: Deutscher Fachverlag.

Yildiz, Erol. 2015. Postmigrantische Perspektiven. In *Nach der Migration. Postmigrantische Perspektiven jenseits der Parallelgesellschaft*. Ed. Erol Yildiz and Marc Hill, 19–36. Bielefeld: transcript.

Yildiz, Erol, and Marc Hill, eds. 2015a. *Nach der Migration. Postmigrantische Perspektiven jenseits der Parallelgesellschaft*. Bielefeld: transcript.

Yildiz, Erol, and Marc Hill. 2015b. Einleitung. In *Nach der Migration. Postmigrantische Perspektiven jenseits der Parallelgesellschaft*. Ed. Erol Yildiz and Marc Hill, 9–16. Bielefeld: transcript.

Zentrum für Globale Fragen an der Hochschule für Philosophie. 2017. Gelingende Wertebildung im Kontext von Migration. Eine Handreichung für die Bildungspraxis. Munich. https://www.kolping.de/fileadmin/user_upload/Projekte/Netzwerk_fuer_Gefluechtete/Material_Download/handreichung_wertebildung.pdf. Accessed: 3 Jan 2022.

Zick, Andreas, und Nora Rebekka Krott. 2021. Einstellungen zur Integration in der deutschen Bevölkerung von 2014 bis 2020. Studienbericht der vierten Erhebung im Projekt Zugleich – Zugehörigkeit und Gleichwertigkeit. IKG – Institut für interdisziplinäre Konflikt- und Gewaltforschung. Bielefeld. https://www.stiftung-mercator.de/content/uploads/2021/08/ZuGleich_Studienbericht_2021_AndreasZick.pdf. Accessed: 3 Jan 2022.

PD Dr. Astrid Wonneberger *Department of Social Work, HAW Hamburg*
As a social and cultural anthropologist, Astrid Wonneberger has been a lecturer in the Applied Family Sciences program at the Hamburg University of Applied Sciences and a private lecturer at the Department of Social and Cultural Anthropology at the University of Hamburg since 2012. After many years of ethnographic field work in the Irish diaspora in the USA and in the Dublin Docklands, her academic interests focus on the topics of family, kinship and *community*, migration, diaspora, ethnicity, and urban anthropology. Since 2018, she has been part of the research team in the BMBF-project POMIKU studying post-migrant family cultures in the Lenzsiedlung in the Hamburg district of Eimsbüttel.

Dr. Sabina Stelzig *Department of Social Work, HAW Hamburg*
After completing her doctorate degree in Sociology on the topic of women's migration, Dr. Sabina Stelzig worked as a research assistant and lecturer in family and migration studies at the University of Hamburg and the Hamburg Institute of International Economics (HWWI). In 2012 she became involved in the development of the Master's program in Applied Family Sciences at the University of Applied Sciences (HAW) Hamburg, where she also teaches Sociology and empirical research methods in the BA Social Work. Since 2018, she has been part of the research team in the BMBF project POMIKU on "post-migrant family cultures".

Diana Lölsdorf, M.A. *Department of Social Work, HAW Hamburg*
Diana Lölsdorf studied Social Work at the University of Applied Sciences Ostfriesland and Family Sciences at the Hamburg University of Applied Sciences (HAW Hamburg). After many years of leadership in early childhood education, she has been working as a research assistant at the HAW Hamburg in the BMBF research project POMIKU (post-migrant family cultures) since 2018.

Prof. Dr. Katja Weidtmann *Department of Social Work, HAW Hamburg*
After her studies in Psychology and Child and Adolescent Psychiatry at the University of Hamburg, Katja Weidtmann worked as a research assistant at the Medical Faculty and at the Clinic for Child and Adolescent Psychiatry, Psychotherapy and Psychosomatics of the University Medical Center Hamburg-Eppendorf. Here she also received her doctorate with an evaluation study of the special outpatient clinic "Giftedness Center". After working as a school psychologist in Lower Saxony and in Hamburg and in a practice for child and adolescent psychiatry and psychotherapy, she became a research assistant at the University of Applied Sciences (HAW) Hamburg in 2012, helped to establish the Master's program in Applied Family Sciences and has been a professor for Family Psychology and Family Counseling since 2016. She is also the head of the Master's program in Applied Family Sciences and of the research project POMIKU.

Do Egalitarian Attitudes Promote Integration?

Gender Role Orientations and Structural Integration of Refugees in Germany

Silke Hans

1 Introduction

Currently, more than three million refugees reside in Germany (Federal Statistical Office 2024a). The large majority of them moved to Germany within the past decade, in particular in the years 2015 and 2016 and in the aftermath of the 2022 Russian invasion of the Ukraine. While the latter group of refugees has been received largely favorably (Moise et al. 2024), public opinion on the considerable number of people seeking asylum in 2015 and 2016 has been and continues to be more divided. Reactions varied from the illustrious "We can do it!" of then-Chancellor Angela Merkel to vehement rejection including xenophobic violence. While the majority of Germans was quite willing to accept refugees from war and civil war areas, skepticism regarding the consequences of such large-scale immigration and the regarding the integration perspectives of refugees was prevalent as well (Gerhards et al. 2016). In part, this skepticism was due to the fact that many asylum seekers came from poor, non-democratic and predominantly Muslim countries, e.g. Syria or Afghanistan. The willingness of the German population to accept immigrants from those areas is less pronounced than towards other immigrants (Hans 2017), in part because of concerns regarding their traditional

S. Hans (✉)
Institut für Soziologie, Georg-August-Universität Göttingen, Göttingen, Germany
e-mail: silke.hans@sowi.uni-goettingen.de

© The Author(s), under exclusive license to Springer Fachmedien Wiesbaden GmbH, part of Springer Nature 2024
A. Wonneberger et al. (eds.), *Values and Value Change in the Post-Migrant Society*, https://doi.org/10.1007/978-3-658-45107-3_2

attitudes and their alleged rejection of values like democracy and gender equality. Likewise, in early 2016, a majority believed that refugees undermine the values central to German society (Gerhards et al. 2016). In reality, empirical evidence shows that approval of democracy and rule of law among refugees is equivalent to the German population, while attitudes towards the role of men and women diverge—less so in the abstract idea of gender equality than regarding specific norms and patterns of behavior (Brücker et al. 2016a, b). Therefore, the question arises whether traditional attitudes and resulting patterns of behavior might impede the incorporation of refugees and especially of refugee women who have come to Germany in recent years.

In this regard, structural integration—the inclusion of refugees in central institutions such as the labor market and education system—is particularly relevant because it affects refugees' immediate economic situation as well as the resulting consequences for their well-being and participation in German society. This is all the more true as the vast majority of refugees in Germany (91 percent) are of school age or employable age (Federal Statistical Office 2023a). According to recent studies, the educational and labor market integration of refugees who arrived in the period around 2015 has already made significant progress (Brücker et al. 2020; de Paiva Lareiro et al. 2020; Gambaro et al. 2020; Graeber and Schikora 2020; Kristen and Spieß 2020). However, there are clear gender differences: women participate less often in qualification measures, have poorer language skills and are much less likely to be employed than men (Brücker et al. 2020; de Paiva Lareiro et al. 2020). Existing studies attribute these differences primarily to the fact that women bring less education and professional qualifications from their respective countries of origin than men and are often prevented from participating in educational institutions and in the labor market due to childcare responsibilities (Brenzel et al. 2017; Brücker et al. 2020; Gambaro et al. 2021; Rother et al. 2017).

The present contribution focuses on an alternative potential cause of gender differences in structural integration, namely, the question to what extent attitudes towards gender roles affect the structural integration of refugees in Germany. Based on data from a representative survey of refugees who applied for asylum in Germany between 2013 and 2016 (IAB-BAMF-SOEP survey, see SOEP 2019),[1]

---

[1] Please note that the present study does not include Ukrainians who were forced to leave their country after the Russian invasion in 2022 and instead concentrates on refugees who came to Germany between 2013 and 2016, many of whom came from countries with very traditional norms and values regarding gender roles.

the results show that attitudes towards gender roles indeed have an effect on the structural integration of women, but not of male refugees. These results provide insights into the specific mechanisms of traditional gender role orientations, which are discussed in the final section of the contribution. First, the following section presents the conceptual framework, the current state of research and the resulting hypotheses.

2 Theoretical Approaches and Empirical Findings on Gender Role Orientations and Structural Integration

2.1 Structural Integration of Refugees and its Explanation

Structural integration of migrants refers to their positioning within the formal institutional system of the host society, particularly in the education system and the labor market, but also the granting of rights, for example, those associated with citizenship. This aspect of integration is particularly relevant because it is associated with access to central resources, such as human capital (knowledge, skills) and economic capital (Esser 2007). Structural integration is therefore closely linked to questions of social inequality—including inequality between different ethnic groups and between women and men.

Regarding the structural integration of recent groups of refugees in Germany, current analyses, which are mainly based on data from the representative IAB-BAMF-SOEP survey, show significant progress in recent years (Kristen and Spieß 2020. For example, the proportion of those with good knowledge of the German language increased from two percent at the time of immigration to 44 percent in 2018 (Brücker et al. 2016a; de Paiva Lareiro et al. 2020). While only three percent of the refugees were employed one year after moving to Germany, 49 percent were employed five years after the move—more than half of them in a qualified job (Brücker et al. 2020). Both adult and minor refugees actively make use of opportunities for general and vocational education or further education in Germany (de Paiva Lareiro et al. 2020; Gambaro et al. 2020). Despite this positive development, the structural integration of refugees tends to proceed more slowly compared to other groups of migrants (Brell et al. 2020).

To explain processes of structural integration, economic or rational-choice-based theoretical approaches, as formulated by Chiswick and Miller 2001 or Esser 2006, have proven helpful. They focus on individual migrants' endowment with and investment in human capital, but they can also integrate structural conditions and non-economic factors. According to these approaches, three aspects affect migrants' educational or labor market success: (1) incentives / motivation, (2) access / opportunity structure, and (3) efficiency. Specific explanatory factors, like age or education, influence structural integration because they affect motivation, access, and/or efficiency. At the individual level, the most important factor is probably the availability of human capital. This includes educational and professional qualifications and skills acquired in the country of origin as well as knowledge of the language of the immigration country. Having such human capital leads to higher efficiency in acquiring further qualifications and facilitates access to labor market positions with higher requirements and better remuneration—in turn a higher incentive for employment. Other explanatory factors at the individual level include migrants' intention to stay in the host country and their family status. Whereas the intention to stay should increase the motivation for structural integration in the host country, migrants' family status can affect both motivation and opportunities for structural integration, for example, due to the time required for childcare. On the other hand, the opportunity structure for labor market integration depends on a variety of factors at the macro level, including the general economic situation, the demand for labor, access to qualification courses and to the labor market, which in turn depends on migrants' legal status. Moreover, discrimination by relevant actors (e.g., public authorities, employers) can impede both access to and the motivation for structural integration. Since many of these factors—in particular legal status, labor market access and language skills—usually change for the better in the years after immigration, structural integration also usually improves over time.

This general explanatory logic also applies to refugees, i.e., their structural integration proceeds similarly and is influenced by the same factors as is the case for other groups of migrants (FitzGerald et al. 2018; Bürmann 2018; Liebau and Schacht 2016). However, refugees differ from other migrants in some particular aspects (FitzGerald and Arar 2018; Brell et al. 2020): In most cases, refugees, who are forced to migrate, have less time to plan and prepare for their move to another country, and often do not get to choose their destination. In consequence, many refugees have no or only very little knowledge of the language spoken in the host country. In addition, many refugees come from countries with a low degree of modernization and therefore have less education and professional qualifications (Brücker et al. 2016a; Liebau and Salikutluk 2016). Once in the host country, language skills and other qualifications may be difficult to acquire while residing in large collective accommodation facilities, worrying about family members and friends in the country of origin, and dealing with the stressful situation before and during forced migration (Gambaro et al. 2018; Walther et al. 2020; Jaschke et al. 2023). Moreover, many asylum seekers are not allowed to take up employment immediately after arrival. Therefore, it is hardly surprising that the structural integration of refugees, while overall similar, often proceeds more slowly compared to other migrants (Brell et al. 2020). This is confirmed by studies on earlier groups of refugees in Germany, which indicate that refugees have lower levels of general and vocational education and of language skills before arriving in Germany, and that they take longer to enter the German labor market and earn less than other migrants (Liebau and Schacht 2016; Liebau and Salikutluk 2016; Salikutluk et al. 2016; Bauer et al. 2017).

2.2 Gender Differences in Structural Integration

In addition to the slower integration compared to other migrants, there are marked differences between men and women.[2] In 2018, 49 percent of male refugees were able to speak German well or very well, but only 39 percent of women without children and 22 percent of women with children (de Paiva Lareiro et al. 2020)—presumably because women responsible for childcare were less likely to attended language courses or make use of other educational opportunities (Brücker et al. 2020). Likewise, employment rates differ significantly between male and female refugees. In 2018, only 13 percent of working-age women were employed, but 45 percent of men; and compared to men, women were significantly more likely to be employed below the level of their professional education or professional activity in the country of origin (Brücker et al. 2020). These differences illustrate the relative disadvantage refugee women in Germany.

The causes for these pronounced gender differences are diverse. Based on the explanatory approach mentioned above, one can argue that incentives, efficiency and opportunities for structural integration are less favorable for women. Female refugees bring less human capital from their home countries—only 56 percent had obtained a school leaving certificate before migration (men: 62 percent) and only 21 percent (men: 26 percent) had any form of vocational training (Brenzel et al. 2017; Brücker et al. 2020). Nineteen percent (men: eleven percent) had never attended a school (Brenzel et al. 2017), and twelve percent of female refugees, but only seven percent of men are illiterate (Rother et al. 2017). For the latter group, integration into the German (vocational) education system and working

---

[2] The studies cited in the following section use the IAB-BAMF-SOEP survey and thus refer to asylum seekers who came to Germany between 2013 and 2016.

life is particularly difficult. Gender differences in work experience before migration are even more pronounced: In their country of origin, three quarters of the men, but only 39 percent of women were employed (Brücker et al. 2020). Another central factor that negatively affects the structural integration and particularly the employment of women is the presence of younger children. By 2018, only 38 percent of women with children under 4 years of age had attended a language course, but about two thirds of men and of women without children or with older children (Rother et al. 2017). At the same time, the presence of younger children reduced the likelihood of employment among women from 13 percent to under five percent, while it had no effect on men (Brücker et al. 2020); likewise, attending a daycare center has positive effects on language skills and structural integration particularly of mothers (Gambaro et al. 2021).

However, considerable differences in employment rates between men and women remain even when differences in human capital and the presence of children are accounted for; moreover, women seem to be able to utilize their education and professional experience acquired in the country of origin less effectively than men (Brücker et al. 2020). This suggests that there are additional reasons for the comparatively low level of structural integration of refugee women. One factor could be gender-related discrimination in the labor market. However, this form of discrimination affects other women (migrants and non-migrants) as well. Since the educational and employment-related differences between men and women are more pronounced among refugees than among the general population, the general mechanisms discussed so far (lack of human capital, childcare, discrimination) cannot entirely explain the relative disadvantage of refugee women. Rather, characteristics specific for the group of refugees might be relevant to explain these pronounced gender differences, for instance, traditional notions of the roles of women and men.

2.3 Traditional Conceptions of Gender Roles as an Impediment to Integration

Gender role orientations[3] (see Davis and Greenstein 2009 for a thorough discussion of the concept) refer to attitudes and beliefs regarding appropriate behavior

---

[3] In the literature, a variety of terms is used to refer to the concept of gender-specific roles and responsibilities: gender ideologies, attitudes towards the equality of men and women etc. (Davis and Greenstein 2009). In this contribution, the terms gender role orientations or attitudes towards gender roles are used primarily.

and (gender-)specific areas of responsibility for men and women. In contemporary western societies, this primarily refers to a distinction between a male-dominated public sphere, e.g. employment or politics, and a female-dominated private sphere (family, household chores, childcare). In other cultural or historical contexts, traditional gender roles may also imply a general superiority of men over women. Gender roles can concern abstract value orientations, i.e. general ideas about what is desirable in a society or for an individual (Hitlin and Piliavin 2004)—in this case regarding the (in-)equality of men and women. They can also refer to concrete attitudes or behavioral norms in specific situations, for example, the division of labor within the family, responsibility for childcare, or participation of women in the labor market. Empirical studies, in particular studies based on modernization theory, usually distinguish between traditional gender role orientations on the one hand and modern or egalitarian ones on the other (see Davis and Greenstein 2009). The former emphasize differences between men and women and see women's responsibility in the private sphere (e.g., household, childcare) and not in employment, while egalitarian attitudes do not make differences between the genders in this respect. Even if recent research shows that gender role orientations are complex and multidimensional (Davis and Greenstein 2009; Knight and Brinton 2017; Barth and Trübner 2018), the relatively simple distinction between traditional and egalitarian orientations has proven useful in empirical studies. The empirical evidence suggests a general decline in traditional and a spread of egalitarian gender role orientations over the past decades—both in Germany and other Western democracies as well as worldwide (Norris and Inglehart 2002; Röder and Mühlau 2014; Pandian 2019).

These changes in attitudes towards the role of men and women do not necessarily go hand in hand with corresponding behavior. Context-dependent discrepancies between value orientations or attitudes on the one hand and actual behavior on the other hand exist in gender role orientations (e.g., Dechant and Schulz 2014; García-Faroldi 2020) as well as in other areas. In particular, abstract value orientations, e.g. support for the general idea of gender equality, are less likely to influence actual behavior than specific attitudes; and the influence of value orientations on actors' motivations is usually stronger than on their actual behavior (cf. Hitlin and Piliavin 2004).

Nevertheless, it is plausible to assume that attitudes towards gender role influence the structural integration of refugee women through various mechanisms. On the one hand, egalitarian gender role perceptions should increase the motivation of women to participate in the German educational system or labor market. There are several reasons for this, some of which directly relate to the content of gender role attitudes: Employment for women and especially married women and mothers with traditional orientations would contradict their own convictions. To avoid cognitive dissonance, traditionally oriented women should prefer to stay at home to take care of their family rather than seek employment outside the home.[4] The motivation to acquire more human capital—for instance, by participating in school, language courses or vocational training—should be lower for women with traditional orientations, as they will not utilize such qualifications in the labor market later on. In addition, traditional attitudes of husbands and other relatives could play a role and negatively affect women's structural integration (Brücker et al. 2016b; Habib 2018), for example, by not encouraging them to pursue an educational degree, by outright forbidding them to work, or simply by not contributing to housework or childcare. Another mechanism should apply to both female and male refugees: Conformity with normative models, values and attitudes dominant in the German population—i.e., egalitarian gender role orientations—should have a positive effect on the sense of belonging and the intention to stay and therefore increase motivation for structural integration. Refugees with traditional gender role orientations, on the other hand, may perceive a cultural distance to and potential conflicts with German society and consequently prefer to return to their country of origin or avoid contact with Germans in the educational system and the labor market. For instance, some men with traditional gender role attitudes would not accept female lecturers or supervisors (see Brücker et al. 2016b). Conversely, the real or perceived distance between refugees and the local population in terms of gender role orientations can also lead to discrimination by relevant gatekeepers in the German population—e.g. teachers or human resource managers—and thereby reduce opportunities for structural integration. This is all the more true since many refugees come from Muslim countries, and negative attitudes towards Muslims are widespread among the German population (Czymara et al. 2017). Again, it is plausible that women are more negatively affected than men are. Muslim women with traditional gender roles are likely to wear a headscarf and are therefore more visible as Muslims (cf. Carol et al. 2015). Finally, the various mechanisms by which gender role orientations may affect structural integration are particularly relevant for those refugees the present study focuses on, namely, those who moved to Germany between 2013 and 2016. The majority of them came from countries where more traditional gender

---

[4] Conversely, to avoid cognitive dissonance, gender role attitudes might change depending on employment status (Corrigall and Konrad 2007; Reichelt et al. 2021; Steiber and Haas 2009).

role orientations prevail and the level of legal equality and of labor market participation of women is low compared to Germany.[5]

Several hypotheses follow from these arguments. Based on the idea that compatibility of values and attitudes between Germans and refugees reduces discrimination and increases the motivation to stay and invest in structural integration, egalitarian attitudes towards gender roles should have a positive effect on the structural integration of male and female refugees in Germany (hypothesis 1). If egalitarian gender role orientations, however, only work because of their substantial content, the positive effect should be limited to women. Therefore, the alternative hypothesis states: Egalitarian gender roles have no impact on the structural integration of male refugees (hypothesis 2). In any case, the positive impact of egalitarian gender role orientations should be stronger in women than in men (hypothesis 3) because of possible interactions of the various mechanisms and because of the potentially stronger influence of third parties (e.g. partners, family members, relevant gatekeepers in German institutions) on women with traditional orientations compared to men.

Since many different factors have an impact on structural integration, the effect of egalitarian gender roles will not be the same for all people and under all circumstances. Research on values and attitudes in other areas, in particular environmental sociology, has shown that attitudes primarily affect behavior in so-called low-cost situations (see Best and Kroneberg 2012). In the context of the present study, the presence of young children represents a high-cost situation with regard to structural integration, as the opportunity for participation in education and employment is severely limited for those who have to provide childcare. Therefore, egalitarian gender role orientations should have a stronger effect on women without children than on women with children (hypothesis 4). Likewise, certain aspects of structural integration are more easily accessible (e.g. learning the German language by participating in an online course) while others require higher costs (e.g. full-time education or employment). Consequently, egalitarian orientations should affect easily accessible aspects of structural integration more strongly than aspects associated with higher costs in terms of time, money, effort, or emotional involvement (hypothesis 5).

---

[5] In 2019, the Gender Inequality Index, a comparative measure of inequality between men and women, which varies between 0 and 1, was 0.084 for Germany (rank 20 out of 162 ranked countries), but much higher for the most important countries of origin of refugees: 0.482 (rank 122) for Syria, 0.545 (rank 138) for Sudan and 0.655 (rank 157) for Afghanistan (UNDP 2020).

The assumption that women's gender role orientations are related to their educational success and labor market activities has been confirmed by empirical studies in different national contexts. For the United States, studies have shown negative effects of traditional gender role orientations on the educational expectations of girls and to a lesser extent of boys (Davis and Pearce 2007), on the employment and income of women, but not of men (Corrigall and Konrad 2007), and specifically on the income level of mothers (Christie-Mizell et al. 2007). Similar relationships were also found in other countries, but were context-dependent (Steiber and Haas 2009). Using panel data, Uunk and Lersch (2019) find that in the United Kingdom, women's labor market activity is influenced by their own gender role attitudes and those of their partners, but not by normative models prevalent in the region of residence. In a comparative study of European countries, Kümmerling and Postels (2020) show that both individual gender role orientations and contextual conditions influence the working hours of women. A positive correlation between egalitarian gender roles and income earned is found by Stickney and Konrad (2007) in a comparative study that includes non-European countries. On the other hand, there seems to be no correlation between gender role orientations and the low employment rates of women in Muslim countries (Abdelhadi and England 2019). There are also empirical findings on the effects of gender role orientations specifically among migrants. Apgar and McManus (2019) find that traditional gender roles, institutions and patterns of behavior in the countries of origin have a negative effect on the labor market integration of second-generation immigrant women in the USA. Likewise, gender role orientations affect the labor market integration of Muslim immigrant women in the Netherlands (Blommaert and Spierings 2019).

3 Data and Methods

To analyze the impact of gender roles on structural integration of refugees in the German context, secondary data from the IAB-BAMF-SOEP survey of refugees (SOEP 2019)[6] are used. The IAB-BAMF-SOEP survey is a representative panel survey of refugees who applied for asylum in Germany between 2013 and 2016, with a sample drawn from entries in the Central Register of Foreigners (AZR). In

---

[6]The data is provided by the SOEP Research Data Center at DIW Berlin. For more information see Giesselmann et al. (2019); Kroh et al. (2016).

each of the yearly surveys, all (adult) household members are interviewed. The present study makes use of the first three waves, conducted between 2016 and 2018. The analyses are limited to refugees who moved to Germany between 2013 and 2016 and who were aged 18 to 64 at the time of the interview. These criteria are met by 7732 respondents (3129 women, 4603 men), of whom 3105 were interviewed once, 2912 twice and 1715 in all three waves. Since different dependent variables and survey waves are used in the analyses, the number of cases varies depending on the respective missing values.

Nine indicators are used to measure four different aspects of *structural integration*: (a) investment in qualifications required on the German labor market, (b) proficiency in the German language, (c) current employment status, and (d) activities planned in the future. (a) To measure investment in human capital, four indicators were available at the time of the first interview: attendance of language or integration courses ($0 =$ no, $1 =$ at least one course), other activities to acquire German language skills, e.g. through friends, media consumption, self-study courses etc. ($0 =$ no, $1 =$ at least one activity), the average daily time spent acquiring German language skills (in hours per day) and the time for other learning or educational activities (including training and further education, also in hours per day). (b) Proficiency in the German language is actually an indicator of successful cultural integration, but at the same time represents a crucial resource for structural integration, especially for educational and labor market success. In the IAB-BAMF-SOEP survey, language proficiency is measured based on respondents' self-assessment in the areas of speaking, writing and reading—each on a five-point scale between "no" and "very good" skills. From this, an index was calculated based on the average value in the three areas. German language skills are assessed in each wave of the survey; in the present study; information from the last available survey for each respondent is used. Since the vast majority of refugees had no knowledge of German before their arrival in Germany, the results at the last survey point represent the competence acquired since arrival. (c) For most refugees, taking up employment is not possible immediately after arrival—be it due to lack of language skills or lack of legal access to the labor market. Therefore, information on respondents' employment status is taken from the last available survey wave. The corresponding variables used in this study differentiate between two ($0 =$ not employed, $1 =$ employed, regardless of extent) or three ($0 =$ not employed, $1 =$ part-time, training, internship etc., $2 =$ full-time) forms of employment. (d) Three indicators are available to measure future behavioral intentions. Respondents who were not employed at the time of the (last) survey were asked about their future employment intentions ($0 =$ unlikely / definitely not, $1 =$ likely / definitely). In the first survey wave, all respondents were asked to indicate how likely they were to take up a job or self-employment and to attend a school, start training or complete a degree in Germany. This information—originally on a scale between 0 (definitely not) and 10 (definitely)—was summarized into two new indicators "probability of employment in Germany" (highest value of the first two items) and "probability of education in Germany" (highest value of the last three items).

Respondents' attitude towards gender roles is the *central explanatory variable*. Six different items are available, all from the initial survey. Respondents were asked to what extent they agreed with the following statements: (1) equal rights for men and women are part of democracy, (2) having a job is the best way for a woman to be independent, (3) even a married woman should have a paid job to be financially independent, (4) if a woman earns more than her partner, it leads to problems, (5) to parents, higher education or vocational training for their sons should be more important than for their daughters, (6) the husband should always have the final say at home. The first item was measured on an eleven-point scale, the others on seven-point scales. A new gender role index represents the average of all items, with the scaling of the first item adjusted and all items recoded so that low values represent a traditional and higher values an egalitarian conception of gender roles. Respondents with missing values were excluded.[7] Although gender role attitudes were available only in the initial survey, the corresponding values for each respondent were imputed in later waves of the survey for the purpose of the present study because some of the dependent variables were taken from later survey waves. This is acceptable because according to the theoretical assumption, attitudes causally precede structural integration (Corrigall and Konrad 2007) and because although attitudes may be subject to changes in the course of life (Davis and Greenstein 2009), they are generally relatively stable over the short periods considered here (two years between the first and last survey wave

---

[7] Attitudes towards gender roles are multi-dimensional (Davis and Greenstein 2009; Knight and Brinton 2017; Barth and Trübner 2018). For instance, a factor analysis of the items used in this study show that items 2 and 3 form a dimension that represents the attitude towards the employment of women. Recent studies show that there are different constellations of these attitude dimensions, each with specific explanatory patterns (Knight and Brinton 2017). In this sense, the idea of gender roles as a one-dimensional construct between traditional and modern / egalitarian ideas is outdated. Nevertheless, a comprehensive scale is used in this study, as the focus in not on effects of a specific aspect—such as attitudes towards employment—but on effects of gender role orientations in general. Also, the internal consistency of the scale is acceptable (Cronbach's alpha $= 0.55$) and the scale is recommended in this form for the IAB-BAMF-SOEP sample (Jacobsen et al. 2018).

at most). In descriptive tables, respondents with traditional gender role attitudes (values from 0 to 3 of the original scale) are distinguished from those who tend towards egalitarian roles (values above 3, but below 6), and those with completely egalitarian attitudes (value 6). For all regression models, the original (continuous) gender role scale was used, but centered at the median value (5) to estimate interaction effects.

Additional *explanatory variables* include gender and the presence of younger children (under 6 years of age) in the household, measured via dummy variables that distinguish four groups of respondents: women without young children, women with young children, men without young children, and men with young children. Some descriptive analyses distinguish between men and women only, regardless of the presence of children.

Control variables for multivariate analyses include respondents' level of education (based on ISCED categories: primary level, lower secondary level, upper secondary level, post-secondary / tertiary education; respondents still in the education system are excluded), the presence of a partner in the household (depending on gender), age, length of stay in Germany, legal status (dummy variables: decision on asylum application still pending, protection status granted, temporary suspension of deportation, other), and the country or region of origin. For age and length of stay, quadratic terms are included in the models to capture nonlinear effects. In models explaining employment, German language proficiency is also controlled.

In the following sections, a comparison of the structural integration of female and male refugees is followed by gender-specific analyses of the effects of gender role attitudes. Bivariate descriptive results are reported for each of the nine indicators of structural integration, followed by linear and logistic regression models for four selected indicators.

4 Results

4.1 Structural Integration of Refugee Women and Men

Table 1 provides an overview of different indicators of structural integration of refugees who came to Germany between 2013 and 2016: investments in human capital, language skills, current employment, and activities planned in the future. To understand the results—and possibly compare them to findings for other groups of migrants—we have to keep in mind that the respondents had only recently arrived in Germany. The average length of stay is only about 1.5 years at

Table 1 Structural integration by gender

	Women	Men	N (Women / Men)
Investment in relevant qualifications			
Attendance of language/integration course (at least one) [a]	57.6%	72.2%	2996/4429
Alternative activities to learn German (at least one) [a]	82.1%	88.4%	1621/2681
Time spent on learning German (hours per day) [a]	2.6	3.3	2646/4126
Time spent on (further) education, learning (hours per day) [a]	0.8	1.4	3027/4457
Proficiency in German			
German language skills (average) [b]	1.8	2.2	3090/4552
German language skills [b]			
practically none	12.1%	5.4%	3090/4552
some	59.9%	54.4%	
(very) good	28.0%	40.2%	
Employment status			
Employment [b]			
not employed	90.2%	64.5%	3111/4582
part-time / training / internship etc.	8.2%	17.4%	
full-time employment	1.6%	18.1%	
Future activities			
Intention to be (self-)employed (likely/certain) [b] [c]	88.1%	96.5%	2812/3179
Probability of school/training/university in Germany (1–10) [d]	6.0	7.0	1566/2612
Probability of employment in Germany (scale: 1–10) [d]	5.5	7.3	1533/2588

a) at the time of the first survey; b) at the time of the last survey; c) only non-employed; d) available only in the initial survey 2016.

the time of the first survey and 2.6 years at the time of the last survey. Considering this, the level of German language skills and the proportion of respondents who are already active in the labor market is quite high. This confirms the findings of previous studies, which show that refugees do not differ significantly in the course of their structural integration from other groups of migrants (e.g. Bürmann 2018). However, as expected, there are significant differences between men and women. This applies, albeit to varying degrees, to all indicators considered. Thus, women do invest in their German language skills and other qualifications, but spend less time doing so than men. Particularly, they are less likely to attend a language or integration course, whereas there are fewer differences between the genders in other—more accessible, but less effective—activities for acquiring German language skills (e.g. self-study courses). Accordingly, it is not surprising that female refugees are somewhat less proficient in the German language than men are. In particular, the proportion of women with good or very good German language skills is only 28 percent, while it is more than 40 percent for men. Furthermore, compared to men, twice as many women do not speak or understand German at all.

It is hardly surprising that the differences are even more pronounced when it comes to employment. At the time of the last interview, more than 35 percent of male refugees are active in the labor market in some form. About half of these men are employed full-time; the rest are working part-time, are in training or doing an internship. On the other hand, more than 90 percent of women are not employed and only a vanishingly small proportion are in full-time employment. The data on activities planned in the future, however, indicate that the women themselves do not wish to be excluded from the labor market: 88 percent of women who are currently not employed intent to pursue employment in the future; for men, the figure is even higher. Combined with the data on actual employment status, the results show that about eleven percent of women and only two percent of men have no intention to work in Germany in the future. Likewise, compared to men, less women expect to participate in an educational program in Germany (e.g. school, vocational training or university).

4.2 Effects of Gender Role Orientations

The analyses in the following sections will reveal to what extent these considerable gender differences in structural integration are due to the prevalence of traditional gender role orientations among refugees, which restrict women and particularly mothers to the private sphere and envisage men as providers and head of the family.

In line with previous studies (Brucker et al. 2016a; Fuchs et al. 2021), the data in Table 2 show that refugees' gender role attitudes hardly differ from those prevalent in the German population. On a scale from 0 (very traditional) to 6

Table 2 Gender role orientations in female and male refugees

	Women (N=2584)	Men (N=3851)
Mean value (scale from 0 to 6)	5.0	4.7
Distribution by category		
traditional (0 to 3)	5.8%	9.3%
rather egalitarian (>3 and <6)	67.1%	72.4%
egalitarian (6)	27.1%	18.3%

(completely egalitarian), women have an average value of 5, and men's average is only slightly less (4.7). The distribution of attitudes towards gender roles is skewed with only a small minority of respondents—about six percent of women and nine percent of men—in the lower to neutral range of the scale (values from 0 to 3), which indicates traditional attitudes. The vast majority, on the other hand, tend to have egalitarian attitudes. 27 percent of women and 18 percent of men score the highest possible value for all six items, and consequently reach value 6 (completely egalitarian) on the comprehensive gender role scale. This response behavior may in part be due to the perceived social desirability in the interview situation. Still, we can conclude that the comparatively lower structural integration of female refugees is not primarily due to traditional conceptions of gender roles. These are simply too rare among refugees to be considered the sole or primary cause; and in particular, women seem to be more egalitarian than men.

However, traditional attitudes could still inhibit structural integration for the minority of women who hold such attitudes. Moreover, qualitative studies show that agreement to a general and abstract notion of gender equality can go hand in hand with traditional attitudes towards behavioral norms in specific situations and corresponding patterns of behavior (Brücker et al. 2016b). Therefore, despite the widespread egalitarian orientations among refugees, it cannot be ruled out that traditional attitudes affect women's structural integration. Figures 1 and 2 provide preliminary evidence for such an effect. They show (for the female and male respondents, respectively) the extent of structural integration depending on gender role orientations. Respondents are classified as either traditional, rather egalitarian, or completely egalitarian.

Across all indicators, a clear correlation between women's gender role orientations and their structural integration is obvious, albeit to varying degrees. Thus, women with egalitarian views spend an average of three hours per day to learn the German language and another hour on other educational activities,

Do Egalitarian Attitudes Promote Integration?

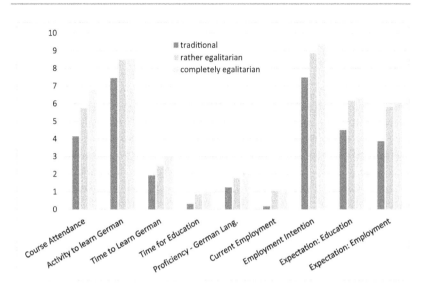

Fig. 1 Structural integration by gender role attitudes (women). *Source:* Figure created by the author

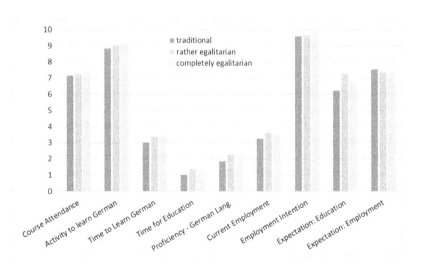

Fig. 2 Structural integration by gender role attitudes (men). *Source:* Figure created by the author

while women with traditional gender roles spend less than two hours on language acquisition and only about 20 minutes on other educational activities. Accordingly, they have fewer German language skills than women with egalitarian attitudes—the difference is almost one point on the scale from 0 (no knowledge) to 4 (very good German language skills). Regarding employment and future behavioral intentions, differences are particularly evident between traditionally oriented women on the one hand and those with rather or completely egalitarian orientations on the other. While only 1.6 percent of women with traditional gender roles are integrated into the labor market in any form, more than 10 percent of the more egalitarian women work at least part-time. Likewise, there are marked differences between both groups of women regarding their expectation to pursue an education or work in Germany. However, even among non-working women with traditional gender role attitudes, about three quarters plan to take up employment in the future. Although there is a clear difference to women with egalitarian attitudes (only six percent have no intention to work), the inclination to work is quite high among refugee women overall. Nevertheless, in the case of women, there is some evidence for a positive effect of egalitarian gender roles on structural integration.

In accordance with hypotheses 2 and 3, the effects of gender role attitudes are clearly more pronounced among women than among men (see Fig. 2). For male refugees, many indicators show only a very slight correlation between gender role attitudes and structural integration, or no correlation at all. Regarding hypotheses 4 and 5, the bivariate findings reported in Figs. 1 und 2 do not initially suggest that gender role orientations are primarily relevant in low-cost situations. For instance, the differences between women with traditional attitudes and women with egalitarian attitudes are more pronounced in the case of employment than in the case of language skills; and they are more pronounced in the case of language course attendance, which requires higher costs in terms of time and effort, compared to alternative lower-cost activities for learning the German language.

In the following sections, multivariate analyses will reveal whether gender role orientations still have an effect on structural integration when other variables are taken into account; in particular, differences between women with traditional and egalitarian attitudes in terms of human capital and family situation. This is important because some factors influence both structural integration and gender role orientations. For instance, respondents who had obtained a high-level educational degree in their country of origin are at the same time more likely to have egalitarian attitudes, to invest in more qualifications, to have better language skills and a higher propensity to work than those who are less educated. Therefore, the higher level of structural integration among egalitarian women might simply be due to their higher level of education, and not to the gender role attitudes themselves. To

Do Egalitarian Attitudes Promote Integration?

Table 3 Effects of gender role orientations: regression models

	Attendance of Language / Integration Course [a]	Proficiency in German Language [b]	Employment [c]	Employment Intention [c]
Woman, child <6 in household [d]	0.44 ***	−0.39 ***	0.46 ***	0.89 ***
Man, no child <6 in household [d]	1.05 ***	0.04	3.64 ***	2.71 ***
Man, child <6 in household [d]	0.93 ***	−0.03	2.00 ***	1.74 ***
Egalitarian gender role	1.33 ***	0.10 ***	1.14 ***	1.44 ***
IA egalitarian gender role*				
Woman, child <6 in household	0.95 ***	0.05	0.81 ***	1.27 ***
Man, no child <6 in household	0.72 ***	−0.02	0.82 ***	0.93 ***
Man, child <6 in household	0.74 ***	−0.04	0.76 ***	0.79 ***
Partner in household	1.21 ***	0.15 ***	0.95 ***	1.11 ***
IA woman * partner in household	0.69 ***	−0.22 ***	0.95 **	0.41 ***
Education: lower secondary [e]	1.51 ***	0.39 ***	1.23 ***	2.49 ***
Education: upper secondary [e]	1.90 ***	0.48 ***	1.47 ***	3.23 ***
Education: postsec./tertiary [e]	2.86 ***	0.76 ***	1.14 ***	3.86 ***
German language proficiency			1.51 ***	
Age in years	1.03 ***	−0.08 ***	1.21 ***	1.16 ***
Age squared	1.00 ***	0.00 ***	1.00 ***	1.00 ***
Duration of stay in years	2.80 ***	0.58 ***	5.17 ***	1.53 ***
Duration of stay squared	0.83 ***	−0.06 ***	0.84 ***	0.96 ***

(continued)

Table 3 (continued)

	Attendance of Language / Integration Course [a]	Proficiency in German Language [b]	Employment [c]	Employment Intention [c]
Constant	0.50 ***	2.75 ***	0.00 ***	1.48 ***
N	5937	5963	5963	4674
(Pseudo) R ^{2}	0.102	0.361	0.209	0.266

a) year of first survey, logistic regression; b) year of last survey, OLS model; c) year of last survey, logistic regression, employment intention: only non-employed; d) reference category: women without child under 6 years; e) reference category: primary education or less; logistic models: odds ratios are reported; all models: gender roles were centered at the median value 5 to calculate interaction variables; controlled, but coefficients not reported: legal status, country of origin; * $p < 0.05$, ** $p < 0.01$, *** $p < 0.001$.

see whether this is the case, multivariate regression models (see Table 3) are estimated for four dependent variables (one for each aspect of structural integration). They include gender, the presence of young children in the household and gender role attitudes as explanatory variables and control for the presence of a partner in the household, the educational level of respondents, their age, the length of stay, the legal status, the country of origin and—in the case of employment as a dependent variable—knowledge of the German language. An OLS model was used to explain proficiency in the German language and binary logistic regression models were estimated for the remaining three indicators (attendance of language/integration courses, current employment, employment intention).

Before the effects of gender role attitudes are discussed in detail, some remarks on the general findings of the regression models: The results reported in Table 3 reveal that the model fit is acceptable in all cases. The explanatory power is lowest for course attendance with a pseudo-R^2 of about 10 percent. In the employment model, pseudo-R^2 is 21 percent, in the case of employment intention even 27 percent. In addition, 36 percent of the differences between the respondents in German language skills can be explained by the variables in the model. Across models, the control variables have effects that were expected. The higher their level of education, the more likely respondents are to attend a language course, to work or intend to work and the higher is their proficiency in the German language. Language proficiency, along with education, also has a strong positive effect on the probability of employment. The probability of attending a language or integration course, of being employed or intending to be employed increases with age, albeit not in a linear way—the effect becomes smaller with increasing age. Younger respondents, on the other hand, are more proficient in the German language. Similarly, the duration of stay has a non-linear effect, which is much stronger than the age effect. With increasing duration of stay, structural integration increases in all areas, especially in the first years. The effects of the duration of stay on employment and on language proficiency are particularly pronounced.[8] The family situation also plays a role, especially for women. While men who live with a partner in the same household attend language courses slightly more often, have slightly higher language skills, and are more likely to intend to work (but slightly less likely to be employed at the time of the interview) compared to men without a partner, the reverse is true for women. For women, the presence of a partner has a negative effect on structural integration across all indicators—particularly on employment intentions. In addition, the having younger children in the household has an even stronger effect. Four groups of respondents were distinguished: women without children under 6 years in the household form the reference category to which the other groups can be compared. Coefficients were estimated for women with young children in the household, men without young children, and men with young children in the household. The level of structural integration is significantly lower for women with young children compared to women without children. Thus, (for women with a value of 5 on the gender role scale[9]) their odds of attending a language course and of being employed are only half compared to women without children. Future employment intentions also decrease with the presence of children; and the average proficiency in the German language is 0.4 points lower than for women without young children. Men—whether with or without children—hardly differ from women without children in terms of course attendance and language skills, but are more often employed or intend to be employed. Like women, they are less likely to be employed when young children live in their household, but the effect is not as strong as it is in the case of female refugees.

Now, how do gender role attitudes affect structural integration when other factors like education and duration of stay are accounted for in the models? To

---

[8] Please note that the analyses are cross-sectional and do not make use of the panel structure of the data. Therefore, the effect of the duration of stay could be partly distorted by other factors, e.g. selective return migrations (see Hans 2010).

[9] For the interpretation of the gender-specific effects of the presence of children, both the reported main effects and the interaction with gender roles must be considered. Since the gender role variable was centered at the median value 5, the main effects (e.g. the odds ratio of 0.44 for women with young children in the language course model) apply to persons with the value 5 (rather egalitarian) on the gender role scale.

assess how such attitudes work for specific groups of refugees, interaction effects with the dummy variables for gender and the presence of children were included in addition to the main effect of gender roles. This way, specific effects for women and men with and without young children can be estimated. In all models, the coefficient of the gender role variable indicates the impact of gender role attitudes in women without young children in the household; for the other groups, the interaction effect must be added to main effect of the gender role variable.

Since the coefficient of the main gender role variable is positive across all models, we can conclude that for women without young children, there is a positive effect of egalitarian gender roles on all indicators of structural integration. With each additional point on the gender role scale (which has a range from 0 to 6, with most respondents scoring well above 3), German language skills increase by 0.1 points, and the odds of attending a language course increase by 33 percent, the odds of employment by 14 percent, and the odds of intending to be employed in the future increase by 44 percent. Since these effects are difficult to interpret in their entirety, especially in the logistic regression models, they are graphically illustrated in Fig. 3 for each model and for each group. The solid black line shows the—consistently positive—effects for women without children. It is obvious that the differences between women with traditional and women with egalitarian attitudes are quite pronounced, even if we ignore the left-hand side of the graphs (values below 3, which are not very common). Between women with rather traditional attitudes (value 3 on the gender role scale) and very egalitarian women (value 6), there is a 16 percentage point difference in the probability of course attendance, a 4 percentage point difference in the probability of employment, a 7 percentage point difference in employment intentions, and a 0.3 scale point difference in German language skills.

Women with younger children in the household have a lower level of structural integration across all indicators—the estimated values (black dashed lines) are below those for women without children.[10] Secondly, egalitarian conceptions of gender roles have less of an effect on course attendance and employment than for women without younger children—the interaction effects are negative and the

---

[10] Since values below 2 on the gender role scale hardly ever occur in practice (less than one percent of the respondents), the estimated values in this range of the scale (e.g. the seemingly slightly higher employment of mothers with a gender role orientation of 0 compared to women without children) are more of a theoretical nature and differences between groups are not statistically significant. The focus in the interpretation should be on the middle and the right-hand side of the respective figures.

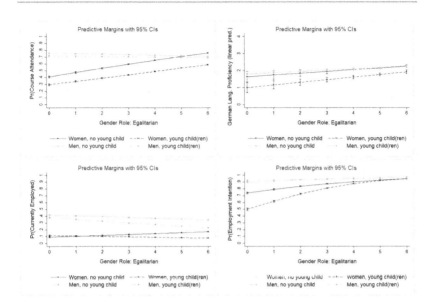

Fig. 3 Effects of gender role attitudes by gender and presence of children. *Source:* Figures created by the author

slopes of the respective lines are not as steep. In the case of employment, there is no positive effect of egalitarian gender roles for women with younger children, i.e., mothers with egalitarian attitudes are no more often employed than mothers with more traditional views. This is in line with hypothesis 4, which assumed that the presence of children represents a high-cost situation in which the effect of attitudes on behavior is limited by other factors—in this case, time required for childcare. However, the same hypothesis is contradicted by the fact that the effect of gender role attitudes on language proficiency does not differ between women with and without younger children—the respective coefficient is not statistically significant. Moreover, the effect of gender roles on employment intentions is stronger among mothers with young children compared to women without children. The latter result could be consistent with the high-cost argument because it suggests that mothers of younger children are more likely than other women to be without employment against their own wishes—many of them intend to take up work as soon as childcare responsibilities no longer stand in the way. For women without (younger) children, non-employment is more likely in line with women's preferences, so that gender role attitudes do not affect future employment intentions as strongly—if they did, employment intentions would have been more likely to be realized in the form of current employment than in the case of mothers. Overall, the findings are ambivalent with respect to hypothesis 4. However, they do support hypothesis 5, which assumed a stronger impact of attitudes towards gender roles with respect to (future) behavioral intentions and the acquisition of qualifications than on actual employment behavior. Indeed, the effect of egalitarian gender role attitudes is strongest in the case of employment intentions, followed by language course attendance. The effect on actual employment is significantly smaller and is not present at all in women with younger children.

For male refugees, the coefficients reported in the table and the grey lines shown in the figures reveal that the level of structural integration is higher for men than for women across all indicators. Only women without children who hold very egalitarian views of gender roles reach the same level in some aspects of structural integration (language acquisition and proficiency). Second, unlike it was the case for women, the presence of children hardly seems to affect male refugees. For three out of four indicators, men with and without younger children do not differ in terms of the level of structural integration nor in terms of the effect of egalitarian gender roles. There is only one exception: Fathers are less likely to be employed than men without young children, especially if they are egalitarian-minded. Possibly, these men are actually more involved in childcare. Finally, egalitarian attitudes towards gender roles in men, unlike women, do not have a consistently positive effect on structural integration. With the exception of language proficiency, which is positively affected by egalitarian gender roles among all groups, the interaction effects for men are consistently negative and counteract the positive main effect of egalitarian gender role attitudes. The likelihood of attending a language or integration course hardly differs between men with traditional and egalitarian views of gender roles, and the employment intention is only slightly higher in men with egalitarian attitudes. In the case of actual employment, egalitarian attitudes even have a negative effect; especially in fathers of younger children. This does not necessarily contradict the findings for women, as traditional gender roles emphasize the role of men as the family's breadwinner outside the home.

Overall, the findings support hypotheses 2 and 3, while there is no evidence for hypothesis 1 in the case of male refugees. There is no universal positive effect of egalitarian gender roles attitudes on the structural integration of men, but there is for women. Consequently, value consensus between refugees and the majority of the German population is probably not the primary mechanism by which egalitarian gender roles affect structural integration. In this regard, the assumption was that refugees who agree with the values and norms prevalent in the host country would have a higher sense of belonging, a higher intention to stay in

Germany (and therefore strive for structural integration), and would suffer less discrimination by the German population. If this were the case, there should be a positive relationship between egalitarian gender roles and structural integration for both women and men.[11] Instead, the specific contents of egalitarian gender roles, which emphasize the relevance of education and employment for women, seem to be relevant and increase women's motivation for activities outside the home, investment in qualifications, and employment, while not affecting men in the same way. In addition, the opportunity structure plays a role: When external restrictions or high costs (e.g., in terms of money, time, or effort) are involved, gender role orientations have less of an impact on women's structural integration.

5 Summary and Discussion

The present study analyzed the effects of gender role attitudes on the structural integration of refugees in Germany. It was assumed that egalitarian attitudes increase the motivation and access to education and labor market integration for both genders, but to a greater extent for women than for men. In addition, gender role orientations should have a stronger impact in low-cost compared to high-cost situations. These assumptions were tested using representative data from the IAB-BAMF-SOEP survey of refugees in Germany, focusing on four aspects of structural integration: investment in human capital, knowledge of the German language, employment status, and future intentions or expectations regarding education and employment. The results confirm a higher level of structural integration among women with egalitarian gender role attitudes compared to women with traditional attitudes, even when controlling for other variables such as education and family status. However, the relationship between gender role orientations and structural integration is complex: It is stronger in relation to behavioral intentions than actual behavior and weaker in the "high-cost" area of employment. The effects of egalitarian attitudes towards gender roles on attending qualification courses and especially on employment are stronger for women without younger children compared to mothers with childcare responsibilities. However, the effects of gender role orientations on employment intentions are stronger for

---

[11] Since there is no such positive correlation for men, we can also rule out a reversed causal relationship. If the attendance of language and integration courses, the mastery of the German language or integration into a German working environment caused egalitarian gender role attitudes (and not vice versa), this effect would show in men as well as in women.

mothers than for women without young children. Finally, no consistently positive effects of egalitarian role orientations on structural integration were found for men.

These findings provide important insights into the possible causal mechanisms of traditional gender role orientations. The fact that traditional views contradict the prevailing ideals and views on gender equality in Germany does not seem to play a role. Apparently, it does not reduce the motivation (by way of intentions to leave Germany) or opportunities (by way of discrimination) for structural integration among those with traditional gender role attitudes. Rather, the specific views associated with traditional or egalitarian orientations are more relevant. According to traditional gender roles, women should be limited to the private sphere and the family, while men are responsible for activities outside the home, such as paid employment. For women with traditional attitudes, such an activity would contradict their own values and preferences. Therefore, they have lower employment intentions, are less often employed, and have less motivation to invest in relevant qualifications or in skills that are only useful outside their own family or household. This is especially true for women with younger children, whose care, according to traditional views, should primarily be in the hands of the mothers. For women with egalitarian views, on the other hand, activities outside the home and gainful employment are in line with their own preferences. Accordingly, they have a higher motivation to invest in relevant qualifications. Whether this motivation can actually be translated into corresponding behavior depends on the respective opportunity structure. The presence of younger children and the lack of childcare alternatives (e.g. daycare facilities) is a significant restriction that prevents women from participating in (further) education and in the labor market. Egalitarian gender role orientations alone cannot counteract these restrictions, even if they increase women's motivation for education and employment. It seems that egalitarian attitudes have a positive effect on actual behavior patterns only when there are no other hard restrictions.

One alternative causal mechanism was not explicitly analyzed in the present study: the impact of relevant third parties on women's motivation and opportunities for structural integration. For migrant and non-migrant women alike, labor market integration often depends on the attitudes and actual behavior of their husbands or partners, for example, their partner's gender role orientation and willingness to engage in childcare (see, for example, Dechant and Schulz 2014; Uunk and Lersch 2019). This mechanism is probably even more pronounced for women with traditional attitudes. These women are particularly likely to have partners or (male) relatives who themselves have traditional attitudes on gender roles and correspondingly have reservations about their wives, daughters or sisters participating in activities outside the home, such as education or paid employment, and at the same time see their own role as heads of families ruling over women (see Brücker et al. 2016b; Habib 2018). They could therefore exert pressure on female family members and thereby prevent women's structural integration. Further research should clarify to what extent this is actually the case. Regardless of the specific mechanisms at work, the present study has confirmed a relationship between gender role orientations and the structural integration of refugee women.

So, could traditional gender roles pose a threat to the structural integration of refugee women in Germany? Despite the relationship between gender role attitudes and structural integration, this does not seem to be the case. On the one hand, despite marked differences between women with egalitarian and more traditional attitudes, even women with traditional views show a considerable degree of structural integration considering the short duration of their stay in Germany. Secondly, other factors have a much stronger impact on structural integration, for instance, human capital and the presence of children. Thirdly, there are actually only relatively few women—and men—with clearly traditional orientations. Only four percent of female and six percent of male respondents score below the value of 3, which marks the middle of the gender role scale. Even if this may in part be due to the interview situation: For the majority of refugee women in Germany, a lack of integration due to traditional gender role orientations is not to be expected. Finally, gender-specific explanatory factors for the labor market integration of refugee women are similar to those for other women in Germany. Traditional gender roles will have a negative impact on them as well, and the propensity to work is generally low among women in Germany as soon as they have children. Only 25 percent of married mothers with minor children in Germany are engaged in full-time work and only a third of women with children under 3 years are employed at all, mostly part-time (Keller and Kahle 2018). All in all, traditional gender role orientations are not a pronounced obstacle to the structural integration of refugee women in Germany—at least if their integration makes more progress in the year to come.

References

Abdelhadi, Eman, and Paula England. 2019. Do Values Explain the Low Employment Levels of Muslim Women Around the World? A Within- and Between-Country Analysis. *The British Journal of Sociology* 70 (4): 1510–1538.

Apgar, Lauren, and Patricia A. McManus. 2019. Cultural Persistence and Labor Force Participation among Partnered Second-Generation Women in the United States. *Social Forces* 98 (1): 211–244.

Barth, Alice, and Miriam Trübner. 2018. Structural Stability, Quantitative Change: A Latent Class Analysis Approach towards Gender Role Attitudes in Germany. *Social Science Research* 72: 183–193.

Bauer, Angela, et al. 2017. Migration und Integration. In *Arbeitsmarkt Kompakt*. Ed. Joachim Möller and Ulrich Walwei, 130-140. Bielefeld: IAB.

Best, Henning, and Clemens Kroneberg. 2012. Die Low-Cost-Hypothese. Theoretische Grundlagen und empirische Implikationen. *Kölner Zeitschrift für Soziologie und Sozialpsychologie* 64 (3): 535-561.

Blommaert, Lieselotte, and Niels Spierings. 2019. Examining Ethno-Religious Labor Market Inequalities among Women in the Netherlands. *Research in Social Stratification and Mobility* 61: 38–51.

Brell, Courtney, Christian Dustmann, and Ian Preston. 2020. The Labor Market Integration of Refugee Migrants in High-Income Countries. *The Journal of Economic Perspectives* 34 (1): 94–121.

Brenzel, Hanna, and Yuliya Kosyakova. 2017. Bildung im Herkunftsland. In *Die IAB-BAMF-SOEP-Befragung von Geflüchteten 2016: Studiendesign, Feldergebnisse sowie Analysen zu schulischer wie beruflicher Qualifikation, Sprachkenntnissen sowie kognitiven Potenzialen*. Ed. Herbert Brücker, Nina Rother, and Jürgen Schupp, DIW Berlin: Politikberatung kompakt 123: 20-29.

Brücker, Herbert, Yuliya Kosyakova, and Eric Schuß, eds. 2020. Fünf Jahre seit der Fluchtmigration 2015. Integration in Arbeitsmarkt und Bildungssystem macht weitere Fortschritte. *IAB Kurzbericht* 4/2020.

Brücker, Herbert, et al. 2016a. Forced migration, arrival in Germany, and first steps toward integration. *DIW Economic Bulletin* 48: 541–556.

Brücker, Herbert, et al. 2016b. Geflüchtete Menschen in Deutschland – eine qualitative Befragung. *SOEP Survey Papers* 313: Series C. Berlin: DIW/SOEP.

Bürmann, Marvin, Peter Haan, Martin Kroh, and Kent Troutman. 2018. Beschäftigung und Bildungsinvestitionen von Geflüchteten in Deutschland. *DIW Wochenbericht* 42: 920–928.

Carol, Sarah, Marc Helbling, and Ines Michalowski. 2015. A Struggle over Religious Rights? How Muslim Immigrants and Christian Natives View the Accommodation of Religion in Six European Countries. *Social Forces* 94 (2): 647–671.

Chiswick, Barry R., and Paul W. Miller. 2001. A Model of Destination Language Acquisition: Application to Male Immigrants in Canada. *Demography* 38 (3): 391–409.

Christie-Mizell, C., André, et al. 2007. Gender Ideology and Motherhood: The Consequences of Race on Earnings. *Sex Roles* 57: 689–702.

Corrigall, Elisabeth A., and Alison M. Konrad. 2007. Gender Role Attitudes and Careers: a Longitudinal Study. *Sex Roles* 56 (11): 847–855.

Czymara, Christian S., and Alexander W. Schmidt-Catran. 2017. Refugees Unwelcome? Changes in the Public Acceptance of Immigrants and Refugees in Germany in the Course of Europe's 'Immigration Crisis.' *European Sociological Review* 33 (6): 735–751.

Davis, Shannon N., and Theodore N. Greenstein. 2009. Gender Ideology: Components, Predictors, and Consequences. *Annual Review of Sociology* 35: 87–105.

Davis, Shannon N., and Lisa D. Pearce. 2007. Adolescents' Work-Family Gender Ideologies and Educational Expectations. *Sociological Perspectives* 50 (2): 249–271.

Dechant, Anna, and Florian Schulz. 2014. Scenarios for the Equal Division of Paid and Unpaid Work in the Transition to Parenthood in Germany. *Comparative Population Studies* 39 (3): 615–644.

de Paiva Lareiro, Cristina, Nina Rother, and Manuel Siegert. 2020. Third wave of the IAB-BAMF-SOEP Refugee Survey. Refugees Are Improving their German Language Skills and Continue to Feel Welcome in Germany. *BAMF Brief Analysis* 01/2020.

Esser, Hartmut. 2006. *Language and Integration. The Social Conditions and Consequences of Language Acquisition by Migrants.* Frankfurt/New York: Campus.

Esser, Hartmut. 2007. Does the "New" Immigration Require a Theory of Intergenerational Integration? In *Rethinking Migration: New Theoretical and Empirical Perspectives*, ed. Alejandro Portes and Josh DeWind, 308–341. Oxford, New York: Berghahn Books.

Federal Statistical Office (Destatis). 2024a. *Persons Seeking Protection, by Protection Status*, 2016 to 2023, Nowcast as of February 13, 2024. https://www.destatis.de/EN/Themes/Society-Environment/Population/Migration-Integration/Tables/nowcast-protection-time-series-protections-status.html#fussnote-1-586704.

Federal Statistical Office (Destatis). 2023a. *Demographic Data on Persons Seeking Protection* as at 31 December 2022, last updated March 30, 2023. https://www.destatis.de/EN/Themes/Society-Environment/Population/Migration-Integration/Tables/persons-seeking-protection-land.html#268962.

FitzGerald, David S., and Rawan Arar. 2018. The Sociology of Refugee Migration. *Annual Review of Sociology* 44: 387–406.

Fuchs, Lukas, Yu. Fan, and Christian von Scheve. 2021. Value Differences between Refugees and German Citizens: Insights from a Representative Survey. *International Migration* 59 (5): 59–80.

Gambaro, Ludovica, et al. 2020. Integration of Refugee Children and Adolescents in and out of School: Evidence of Success but Still Room for Improvement. *DIW Weekly Report* 34: 345–354.

Gambaro, Ludovica, Guido Neidhöfer, and C. Katharina Spieß. 2021. The Effect of Early Childhood Education and Care Services on the Integration of Refugee Families. *Labour Economics* 72: 102053. https://doi.org/10.1016/j.labeco.2021.102053.

Gambaro, Ludovica, et al. 2018. Refugees in Germany with Children Still Living abroad Have Lowest Life Satisfaction. *DIW Weekly Report* 42: 415–425.

García-Faroldi, Livia. 2020. Mothers' Autonomy or Social Constraints? Coherence and Inconsistency Between Attitudes and Employment Trajectories in Different Welfare Regimes. *Social Politics* 27 (1): 97–127.

Gerhards, Jürgen., Silke Hans, and Jürgen. Schupp. 2016. German Public Opinion on Admitting Refugees. *DIW Economic Bulletin* 21: 243–249.

Giesselmann, Marco, et al. 2019. The Individual in Context(s): Research Potentials of the Socio-Economic Panel Study (SOEP) in Sociology. *European Sociological Review* 35 (5): 738–755.

Graeber, Daniel, and Felicitas Schikora. 2020. Refugees' High Employment Expectations: Partially Met. *DIW Weekly Report* 34: 337–343.

Habib, Nisren. 2018. Gender Role Changes and their Impacts on Syrian Women Refugees in Berlin in Light of the Syrian Crisis, *WZB Discussion Paper SP* VI 2018-101.

Hans, Silke. 2017. Einstellungen zu Zuwanderern und Flüchtlingen in Europa. *Geographische Rundschau* 3: 38–45.

Hans, Silke. 2010. *Assimilation oder Segregation? Anpassungsprozesse von Einwanderern in Deutschland*. Wiesbaden: VS.

Hitlin, Steven, and Jane A. Piliavin. 2004. Values: Reviving a dormant concept. *Annual Review of Sociology* 30: 359–393.

Jacobsen, Jannes, Julius Klikar, and Jürgen Schupp. 2018. Scales Manual IAB-BAMF-SOEP Survey of Refugees in Germany – revised version. *SOEP Survey Papers 475*: Series C. Berlin: DIW/SOEP.

Jaschke, Philipp, et al. 2023. Mental Health and Well-Being in the First Year of the COVID-19 Pandemic among Different Population Subgroups: Evidence from Representative Longitudinal Data in Germany. *British Medical Journal Open* 13 (2023): e071331. https://doi.org/10.1136/bmjopen-2022-071331.

Keller, Matthias, and Irene Kahle. 2018. Realisierte Erwerbstätigkeit von Müttern und Vätern. Zur Vereinbarkeit von Familie und Beruf. *WISTA* 3: 54–71.

Knight, Carly R., and Mary C. Brinton. 2017. One Egalitarianism or Several? Two Decades of Gender-Role Attitude Change in Europe. *American Journal of Sociology* 122 (5): 1485–1532.

Kristen, Cornelia, and C Katharina Spieß. 2020. Fünf Jahre danach: Eine Zwischenbilanz zur Integration von Geflüchteten. *DIW Wochenbericht* 34: 559–561.

Kroh, Martin, et al. 2016. Das Studiendesign der IAB-BAMF-SOEP-Befragung von Geflüchteten. *SOEP Survey Papers* 365: Series C. Berlin: DIW/SOEP.

Kümmerling, Angelika, and Dominik Postels. 2020. Ist die Geschlechterrolleneinstellung entscheidend? Die Wirkung länderspezifischer Geschlechterkulturen auf die Erwerbsarbeitszeiten von Frauen. *Kölner Zeitschrift Für Soziologie und Sozialpsychologie* 72: 193–224.

Liebau, Elisabeth, and Zerrin Salikutluk. 2016. Many Refugees Have Work Experience but a Smaller Share Possess Formal Vocational Qualifications. *DIW Economic Bulletin* 35: 392–399.

Liebau, Elisabeth, and Diana Schacht. 2016. Language Acquisition: Refugees Nearly Achieve Proficiency Level of Other Migrants. *DIW Economic Bulletin* 35: 400–406.

Moise, Alexandru D., James Dennison, and Hanspeter Kriesi. 2024. European Attitudes to Refugees after the Russian Invasion of Ukraine. *West European Politics* 47 (2): 356–381.

Norris, Pippa, and Ronald Inglehart. 2002. Islamic Culture and Democracy: Testing the "Clash of Civilizations" Thesis. *Comparative Sociology* 1 (3): 235–263.

Pandian, Roshan K. 2019. World Society Integration and Gender Attitudes in Cross-National Context. *Social Forces* 97 (3): 1095–1126.

Reichelt, Malte, Kinga Makovi, and Anahit Sargsyan. 2021. The Impact of COVID-19 on Gender Inequality in the Labor Market and Gender-Role Attitudes. *European Societies* 23 (S1): 228–245.

Röder, Antje, and Peter Mühlau. 2014. Are They Acculturating? Europe's Immigrants and Gender Egalitarianism. *Social Forces* 92 (3): 899–928.

Rother, Nina, Diana Schacht, and Jana A. Scheible. 2017. Sprachpotenziale: Sprachkenntnisse und Alphabetisierungsgrad von Geflüchteten. In *Die IAB-BAMF-SOEP-Befragung von Geflüchteten 2016: Studiendesign, Feldergebnisse sowie Analysen zu schulischer wie beruflicher Qualifikation, Sprachkenntnissen sowie kognitiven Potenzialen [tAB-BAMF-SOEP survey of refugees 2016: study design, field results and analyses of edu-*

cational and professional qualifications, language skills and cognitive potentials]. Ed. Herbert Brücker, Nina Rother, and Jürgen Schupp, *DIW Berlin: Politikberatung Kompakt* 123: 29–41.

Salikutluk, Zerrin, Johannes Giesecke, and Martin Kroh. 2016. Refugees Entered the Labor Market Later than other Migrants. *DIW Economic Bulletin* 35: 407–413.

Socio-Economic Panel (SOEP) 2019. *Data for years1984-2018*, version 35. https://doi.org/10.5684/soep-core.v35.

Steiber, Nadia, and Barbara Haas. 2009. Ideals or Compromises? The Attitude-Behaviour Relationship in Mothers' Employment. *Socio-Economic Review* 7: 639–668.

Stickney, Lisa T., and Alison M. Konrad. 2007. Gender-Role Attitudes and Earnings: A Multinational Study of Married Women and Men. *Sex Roles* 57: 801–811.

UNDP (United Nations Development Programme). 2020. *Human Development Report 2020. The Next Frontier. Human Development and the Anthropocene*.

Uunk, Wilfred, and Philipp M. Lersch. 2019. The Effect of Regional Gender-Role Attitudes on Female Labour Supply: A Longitudinal Test Using the BHPS, 1991–2007. *European Sociological Review* 35 (5): 669–683.

Walther, Lena, et al. 2020. Living Conditions and the Mental Health and Well-being of Refugees: Evidence from a Large-Scale German Survey. *Journal of Immigrant and Minority Health* 22: 903–913.

Prof. Dr. Silke Hans *Institute of Sociology, Georg-August-Universität Göttingen*
Silke Hans is a professor of sociology at Georg-August-Universität Göttingen. Her research focuses on migration, immigrant incorporation, and social inequality. After studying sociology and political science, she became a research assistant at Freie Universität Berlin, where she received her doctorate in 2008, based on a longitudinal study of immigrant incorporation in Germany. From 2018 to 2021, she has been leading subproject 4: "Values and belonging as predictors of integration" of the joint project AFFIN.

Attitudes and Values of Young Men with and Without Migration and Refugee History in Relation to Gender and Equality

Implications for Society and Social Integration in Germany

Silke Remiorz, Katja Nowacki and Katja Sabisch

1 Introduction

The public discourse about shared values and attitudes within the German majority society reached its preliminary peak against the backdrop of increased refugee migration in 2015. Images of people fleeing war, violence, and hunger from Syria, Afghanistan, or Iraq via the Balkan route, seeking protection and refuge in Europe, went viral in the summer of 2015. To avert a looming humanitarian catastrophe in Europe, the federal government under Chancellor Angela Merkel granted several hundred thousand people the opportunity to find protection in Germany and apply for asylum. It seemed that a 'welcome culture' with its associated Christian-influenced basic values of the Federal Republic of Germany was shared by the majority of society at this time, as, for example, the right to asylum

---

S. Remiorz (✉) · K. Nowacki
Fachbereich Angewandte Sozialwissenschaften, Fachhochschule, Dortmund, Germany
e-mail: silke.remiorz@fh-dortmund.de

K. Nowacki
e-mail: katja.nowacki@fh-dortmund.de

K. Sabisch
Gender Studies, Ruhr-Universität, Bochum, Germany
e-mail: katja.sabisch@rub.de

enshrined in the Basic Law (Art. 16a GG) and the implied will of the German population 'to help', was guiding action (BMFSFJ 2017). Thus, Germany can be considered a central country of immigration within the European Union, which, not least due to its own past, views human rights and diversity as important elements of the existing value system. The people, who immigrated to Germany in the 1960s as so-called "guest workers" (Treibel 2003), shaped an ethnically diverse image (Pries 2013). While this societal diversity, according to Elias, could establish itself in large parts, refugees so far remain outsiders (Elias and Scotson 2002), as the high number of asylum seekers arriving in Germany stirs fear of "over-foreignization" in some parts of society (Zick and Küpper 2015).

To classify the understanding of the terms "migration background" and "refugee history", these should be briefly introduced. A person with a migration background is, according to the definition of the Federal Statistical Office (Statistisches Bundesamt 2018a, p. 4), a person, who "either themselves, or at least one parent was not born with German citizenship".[1] People with migration backgrounds are thus "immigrated and non-immigrated foreigners, immigrated and non-immigrated naturalized citizens, (late) resettlers and descendants born with German citizenship of the three previously mentioned groups" (Statistisches Bundesamt 2018a, p. 4). A person with a refugee history is a person who flees due to armed and warlike conflicts in their home country or due to individual political, ethnic, or religious persecution, and out of fear of torture or death cannot return to their home country (United Nations High Commissioner for Refugees 2015). The Federal Government's Expert Commission on the Framework Conditions for Integration Capability (Fachkommission der Bundesregierung zu den Rahmenbedingungen der Integrationsfähigkeit 2020) suggests abandoning the term "migration background" and instead speaking of "immigrants and their (direct) descendants". In the present research project *JUMEN* the terms "refugee and migration background" are still used, as most official statistics refer to this designation.

Looking at the value orientation within a society, this implies according to Thome (2019, p. 47) also the question of whether the values applicable to a society contribute to the integration of certain groups of people—e.g. people with a migration background or with a history of flight—into society, or whether these

---

[1] All statements quoted from sources originally published in German were translated by DEEPL and revised by the authors for accuracy. The same applies for the interviews which were all conducted in German: The passages quoted in this article were translated by DEEPL and revised by the authors.

people are rather stylized as a "source of social conflicts and exclusions". The present study is particularly interested in the prevailing values regarding gender equality within the German majority society from the perspective of young men. The interest is primarily based on the societal debate about young men with a history of flight that arose after the New Year's Eve in Cologne in 2015/2016, which can be considered as "the point of no return" for a changing value discussion in Germany (Ege and Gallas 2019, p. 105). Sanyal (2017) describes the changing value discourse after the incidents on New Year's Eve in Cologne in 2015/2016 as "PostCologneialism", which means that "Cologne" *firstly* symbolically stands for an alleged danger posed by migration and especially by male migrants or refugee men. *Secondly* "Cologne" is representative of a discursive processing of the topic of gender/masculinity in the immigration society, which culturalizes social inequalities and ethnicizes sexism (Huxel et al. 2020). The documented (sexualized) assaults on women on the cathedral square by a large number of young men with a migration and flight history sparked a discussion about existing values and a questioning of immigration and asylum policy. The debate reached its climax with the facilitated deportation policy of (sexual) offenders with the introduction of the Asylum Package II in March 2017 and the expansion of the third country regulation (referring to the Maghreb countries) contained therein by the Federal Ministry of the Interior (Huxel et al. 2020; Werthschulte 2017). However, the discussion about the events of New Year's Eve in Cologne first and foremost contributed to stigmatizing (young) men with a history of flight as a uniform (perpetrator) group. These *Othering* processes lead to a "culturalization of marginalized masculinities" and function as "reinforcements of ethnicization and sexism" (Huxel et al. 2020, p. 128)—without at the same time problematizing (sexualized) violence against women within the German majority society (ibid.).

The 'post-Cologne' debate about young Muslim men thus impressively shows how sexism and sexualized violence against women are ethnicized. For example, it was claimed that "[t]he civil war refugees … are dangerous for German women" and that the "refugees […] have to go away" (Dietze 2016a, p. 93). This shows that physical and sexual violence against women is unilaterally attributed to Muslim men as perpetrators—without considering that origin and religious affiliation are not the parameters that can lead to possible violence against women. In this context, the term "ethno-sexism" is often mentioned, which emphasizes that a "culturalization of gender" takes place, which "discriminates ethnically marked people because of their supposedly special, problematic or 'backward' sexuality or sexual order" (Dietze 2016b, pp. 3–4).

The question of societal diversity and the integration of refugees (Pries 2016) is therefore negotiated not least through gender attributions (Mayer et al. 2016).

Young Muslim men, who represent a majority of the refugees (BAMF 2016), are currently at the center of the discourse on values, they are stigmatized due to their origin, their religion, their gender, and their age (Dietze 2016a). However, sexism and sexual violence against women is a societal problem. In fact, one in three women in Germany has been affected by physical and/or sexual violence at least once in their life, with the suspects in 63.2% of cases having German citizenship (Bundeskriminalamt 2020). According to a study by Schmidt, Pettke, Lehmann, and Dahle (2017, p. 322), male sex offenders with a migration background are less characterized by "sexually deviant interests than by opportunities, group dynamics, and general antisocial readiness to act" than offenders without a migration background. According to Hark and Villa (2017, p. 10), it is therefore a societal obligation to critically engage with the convergence of "racism, sexism, and feminism" within the entire German society. Because a connection of e.g. racism, anti-semitism, and anti-feminism, which is claimed by the interpretive sovereignty of white men, seems to be completely ignored here (Author Collective FE.IN 2020). In particular, men with a migration background are attributed by white men to have different values regarding the image of the white woman than Western societies. However, this accusation is mainly based on the "patriarchal power structure and a modernized anti-feminist agenda, which is based on the desire to restore the dichotomous hierarchical social order" and thus reveals a societal problem, which remains unnoticed here (AK FE.IN 2020). It is therefore easier for certain populist currents to ethnicize sexual violence and ignore crime statistics (e.g. Bundeskriminalamt 2019) that show that sexual violence mostly occurs in the domestic environment.

In previous research, there is little knowledge about the subjective attitudes and values of young men in relation to gender and equality. The aim of the *JUMEN* study, for example, is to use guideline-based qualitative interviews to record the attitudes of young men with and without a migration and refugee history towards gender and equality and to work out the associated values. It is assumed that *attitudes* are to be differentiated from values in two respects, because "a) attitudes are exclusively assigned to individuals, and b) they do not have a should inscribed in them, but only a factually positive, negative or indifferent attitude towards specific objects" (Thome 2019, p. 57). *Values* are described by Kluckhohn (1951, p. 395) as a "concept of the desirable". Schwartz and Bilsky (1987, p. 551) structure human values as follows:

> "values are (a) concepts or beliefs, (b) about desirable end states or behaviors, (c) that transcend specific situations, (d) guide selection or evaluation of behavior and events, and (e) are ordered by relative importance".

Values are therefore a) concepts or beliefs about b) desirable end states or behaviors, which c) go beyond specific situations, d) guide the selection or evaluation of behavior and events, and e) are ordered by relative importance (Bilsky 2015).

According to Schwartz and Bilsky (1987), this structuring should by no means be considered universal or rigid. Values are rather an expression of basic human needs, which refer to biological, social, and societal requirements (Bilsky 2015). Schwartz (1992) designed a simplified value model, the *Schwartz Value Surveys (SVS)*, in which four dimensions of value orientation were focused and the following two simplified "value" contrasts could be identified: 1. The preservation of existing traditions versus openness to change, and 2. the self-overcoming of the individual versus self-elevation or one's own performance and power. He also assumed that human values can be divided into individual and collective value perceptions, which guide the respective actions of individuals and thus also represent the two simplified "value" contrasts (Bilsky 2015). Since the *Schwartz Value Survey* is an internationally evaluated structural model, it also served as a heuristic for capturing implicitly expressed values of young men in the present study.

The subjective attitudes of young men with and without migration and refugee history regarding gender and equality will be classified into the value orientation system according to Schwartz (1992, 2016) using $N=62$ qualitative interviews from the *JUMEN* study. The similarities and differences between the groups in terms of the four dimensions of value orientation will be clarified. This serves, not least, to substantiate the current societal value discussion.

2 Method for Capturing the Attitudes and Implicit Values of Young Men Towards Gender and Equality in the JUMEN Study

The collection of attitudes was carried out through guideline interviews, with the answers dealing with the topic of gender and equality being classified into the value system of Schwartz (1992). The methodological framework of the qualitative part of the *JUMEN* study is listed below. This includes a presentation of the sample as well as the research instrument and the evaluation method.

2.1 Participants of the Study

The present sample consists of a total of $N=62$ young men with and without migration and refugee history, which can be divided into three equally large subgroups. These are $n=20$ German young men without migration and refugee history, $n=21$ young men who have fled, and $n=21$ young men of Turkish origin from the 2nd generation. The young men interviewed were on average 18.7 years old at the time of data collection (SD 3.56, Min 14 Max 27). The acquisition of the interview partners was carried out both through a direct approach of cooperating welfare organizations and through advertisements on social media portals, notices in universities, youth centers, and supermarkets. This was to ensure that the sample was as heterogeneous as possible. The data collection took place at the request of the interview partners either in the rooms of the Dortmund University of Applied Sciences or the Ruhr University Bochum, or in the domestic environment of the interview partners. Some interviews also took place in the cooperating welfare organizations. The interviews were conducted by male interviewers who identified themselves with the respective interviewed subgroup, thereby minimizing socially desirable response behavior as much as possible. The interviews lasted an average of 40 min (min. 25 min, max. 75 min) and were subsequently transcribed verbatim and anonymized. The interview partners were free at all times not to answer questions or to break off the interview. The interviewers were available for open questions afterwards.

2.2 Qualitative Interviews

The present data were collected using a semi-standardized problem-centered interview (Witzel and Reiter 2012). All interviews were conducted in German and the respondents also answered in German. The evaluation of the interviews was carried out using the Qualitative Content Analysis according to Mayring (2015), supported by the use of the MAXQDA 2020 program (VERBI Software 2019). The interview guide contained, among other things, questions about attitudes towards gender, on the subject of equal rights for women and men, and on gender equality (see also Nowacki et al. 2022). In the 'Equality' section of the interview, the following questions and follow-up questions were asked, for example:

"In the media (newspapers or social networks) we read a lot about women earning less money than men and being less frequently found in leadership positions in organizations and companies. What do you think about this? What do you think are the reasons for this? Do you think measures should be taken against this, such as the gender quota or the appointment of equality officers?" After answering these questions about the general attitude towards equality, more specific follow-up questions were asked, e.g.: "How would it be for you if your female partner were in a leadership position?". Questions were also asked about attitudes towards sexual diversity, but this set of questions is not considered in the present analysis of the interviewees' statements (analyses on this in Nowacki et al. 2022).

The statements of the young men interviewed were deductively assigned to the four dimensions of value orientation according to Schwartz (1992, 2016) and analyzed with regard to the categories "gender", "equality", and "gender equality". The evaluation was carried out across all three groups in order to be able to make general statements about the attitudes or values of the young men. It should be noted at this point that all manifestations, both in the negative and in the positive sense with regard to the question, could be found in the statements of the respondents across all three groups. Furthermore, the anchor examples listed in this article are not typical statements that can be assigned to only one group.

3 Results

Based on the dimensions of value orientation according to Schwartz (1992, 2016), anchor examples could be identified in all interviews of the young men interviewed across all three groups, which could be assigned to the respective value dimensions.

3.1 Preservation

The value dimension "Preservation" defined by Schwartz (1992) has three central aspects: 1. Traditions, 2. Conformity, and 3. Security. Traditions, according to Schwartz (2016), include respect, connection, and acceptance of customs and norms that characterize one's own culture or religion. A person's conformity refers to individual "restrictions on actions, inclinations, and impulses that could offend or hurt others or even violate social expectations and norms" (Bilsky 2015, p. 4). A person with a pronounced awareness of conformity, therefore, clearly supports those societal expectations that are directed at them. The last aspect of preservation is security, which includes the "harmony and stability of society" as well as the "harmony and stability of relationships and one's own 'self'" (Bilsky 2015, p. 4).

After analyzing the statements of the young men interviewed from all three groups, it became clear that the preservation of traditions—in the sense of maintaining and accepting a traditional gender and family image—is strongly emphasized by the respondents. It can be noted that the young men interviewed mostly grew up in a traditional family form (married heterosexual couple with at least one biological child). This also corresponds to the most common family form in Germany in 2018 with 68.4 % (Statistisches Bundesamt 2018b). Only a few of the young men interviewed from all groups grew up as an only child in their family. The young men of the group without migration and flight history describe in their statements a situation of growing up with their biological parents and only one other sibling. In the group of young men of Turkish descent and young men with migration and refugee history, most respondents grew up in families with multiple children. Moreover, all respondents from the three groups emphasized that they perceived a traditional division of tasks in family life among their parents. In the statements of the young men, it also became clear that they show a high conformity with the heteronormative and traditional family and gender image they experienced in their family. Based on Oelkers (2012), one can assume a so-called "normal family image" here.

Holding on to these traditional family and gender images can be interpreted as a desire for security on the part of the young men. It could primarily give the young men a feeling of stability and harmony in relation to existing relationships and also towards their own self (Schwartz 2016). Thus, a young man describes the roles his parents played in his upbringing or in family life and the influence the lived roles have on him as an adult young man:

> "My dad always said to my mom: 'Stay at home, take care of the children, help them with school, you are really there for them and I bring home the money'. So and that is the typical role, dad goes to work, mom stays at home. [...] Just this 'you are the man, so you take care, you have this protector role.... And men don't cry, so that's what I have in my head. What has shaped me the most, I think."

The statement makes it clear that the category of gender is considered by the interviewee as a structural category. Thus, not only in the previous statement, but also largely in the statements of the other young men, it is evident that they attribute certain characteristics and actions to the female and the male gender. The justification for the differences strongly extends towards assumed biological differences (men must be strong, therefore they do not cry and take on the protector function) (Degele 2008; Ehlert 2012). In the majority of the statements, it becomes clear that the interviewees grew up in traditional nuclear families in which the preservation of traditional gender images in relation to the care of children and the household was practiced. In most cases, therefore, the fathers of the interviewees are primarily employed and provide for the family income, whereas the mothers are mostly at home and take care of the upbringing of the children.

> "**Who took on which tasks in your upbringing**? My father has always been the one who was working [...] My father was really primarily the worker. So when my mother was out for whatever reason, my father, I would say, continued to work, in quotation marks. But my mother was more involved with the upbringing of both my brother and me. My father was more like, I would say, the sidekick.. **So more passive, right?** Yes, not necessarily passive. There are also active parts. My father was then more responsible for, I would say, the outings, be it to the zoo, be it to the park, be it somewhere else. But my mother was more the carer, if you will."

Here it also becomes clear that fathers seem to be more responsible for leisure activities, which also corresponds to findings of father research (see e.g. Eickhorst and Nowacki 2019; Grossmann et al. 2002). Only a few interviewed young men from all three groups questioned the traditional role distribution within their family. It can be assumed that the described actions are based on an idea of certain societal basic assumptions of gender as a structural category (Degele 2008; Ehlert 2012).

In addition, some of the young men's statements emphasize that they have a high satisfaction with traditionally shaped gender roles. The following interview excerpt makes it clear that the young man interviewed wants to adhere to these traditions in his own family life:

> "Exactly, I did say that, for example, when I'm married, I want to have children. And someone has to look after them. Sure, I could get a babysitter or something, but I wouldn't want that. I would want my wife to raise the children. That's how I learned it, and that's how I would continue. And therefore, of course when the children are grown up, then the question arises. She [his wife, note from the authors] will probably not be able to work full time until they [his children, note from the authors] are adults.... Part-time is still possible, but I wouldn't want her to give up her whole job, unless she really doesn't want to work anymore and look after the children. Then great, she can stay at home. If she wants to work, she should go to work. Because some women really need that as self-affirmation."

It is evident that the young adult has a rather patriarchal view of society, emphasizing that his future partner would have to give up her job for the time of child-rearing and afterwards only if she shows a clear will to go back to work part-time. A fundamental negotiation process about the distribution of family tasks with a potential partner is not considered here, but from the beginning a traditional task assignment is seen as self-evident, which he refers to as 'learned'. His role as a father is not explicitly mentioned in relation to children or a job, it can only be indirectly assumed that he sees his task in the financial provision of the family. The expressed idea of a traditional family model is comparable to the results of the 18th Shell Youth Study. This also shows that the idea of family is rather conservatively shaped (Hurrelmann et al. 2019). Another young man describes in the following example the traditional family life he experienced in his childhood and adolescence and which he does not question. This shows an example of the task distribution within a traditional nuclear family. In terms of role distribution, emotional availability is also hinted at, which is also seen as a classic task of women (Hobler et al. 2017).

> "So my mother was always at home. When I went to school, when I came home, she was always there, the food was always ready. And my father was usually at work. [...] So sometimes my father was also at home when I arrived. So,... my mother talked more with us than my father. More on the level of what we think, what we feel, my mother talked more with us, my father less. My father more for other things."

The preservation of traditions is also evident in statements regarding the employment of women and men. The preservation of traditions is strongly linked to a naturalization of gender, where the physical characteristics and abilities of each gender are cited as the reason for a specific task allocation (Becker-Schmidt 1987). The following quote makes this aspect of the definition of differences between men and women in the profession due to biological differences (muscle strength, pregnancy) clear. However, this example also expresses doubts about the unequal treatment of men and women, which he sees as unfair. This shows an ambivalence in the attitude towards the traditional gender role:

> "So I think it depends on which profession women and men work in, and I believe it is like this, in construction jobs, because there are many women who are not as strong as men and then perform less and therefore less performance I think, is also less money, because of less performance. But this cliché "Yes, she'll get pregnant at some point and then she'll be out forever", that's also quite nonsense. Because sure, it can happen that a woman gets pregnant, but if she is career-oriented, she will also wait for a more favorable time. And (7 sec.) I think, even with leadership positions for example, it doesn't matter who does it. So I think it's not the case that a man should be paid more than a woman. I believe this comes more from the outdated view that the man is stronger than the woman and generally better."

Different physical abilities are mentioned in a majority of the interviews as a reason for lower pay for women in some professions; in addition, the aspect of possible pregnancy is mentioned as a reason why women may not hold leadership positions in certain professions or are not fully employed. However, some young men also reported that their mothers had to work because the family would not have had enough money otherwise. Nevertheless, the mothers were primarily responsible for raising the children in the traditional sense, in addition to their employment. The mothers' professional activity was therefore a financial necessity and was not discussed in terms of the women's natural development or realization.

Only occasionally did some young men state that both parents would work equally and that the distribution of tasks in the household and upbringing between the parents was or is divided equally.

> "So in the past my father was actually at home more than my mother. And because my mother was always at school working and my father is freelance and therefore he could always arrange his jobs so that it fit with picking up from kindergarten or elementary school and so on. And accordingly he was more like the houseman, I would say. And otherwise it's quite balanced. So I wouldn't say that either of the two had a greater influence on the upbringing or anything. Except that I was out and about a bit more with my father earlier. But actually it was very balanced and yes."

However, it generally becomes clear that usually the father worked full-time and the mother part-time or was on parental leave and was thus responsible for raising the children and running the household. This form of employment is reflected in the current figures on the employment of couples with children in Germany, in which around 24% of couples with a child under three years of age follow this model (Federal Statistical Office 2019).

3.2 Openness for Change

In Schwartz's (2016) value orientation, the dimension "Openness for Change" is mentioned contrary to the dimension of preservation. In this, one's own self-control, i.e., the ability of humans to observe, evaluate, specifically reinforce their own behavior, and flexibly align it with their own goals, is central.

Statements from the interviewed participants of all three groups could also be assigned to this dimension. The aspect of gender equality was a central theme, showing a general openness. This is evident in the following example:

> "**What do you think of the measures of the gender quota or the equality opportunity officer?** First and foremost, it's of course great. In the second place, it's absolutely unacceptable that we need something like this at all. It should be regulated from the beginning that women and men are also equal in professions, meaning that men do not think superficially and prejudiced. Accordingly, I think, the wom-

en's quota or gender quota in general is great, but actually it should not exist at all, because from the beginning people should be equal and be treated equally."

Even in the following example, there is still a certain openness for change in the sense of acceptance of women in leadership positions evident. However, there is also a direct expression of concern that this could lead to a shift in power relations within the private relationship.

> "**But imagine you have a girlfriend, and she would now be the boss, would be in a leadership position. How would you find that?** Well, if she, let's say, at home does not try to put herself above me and we talk to each other on one level and everything, then I would have no problem with that. So, it's nice if she somehow earns money maybe **(laughs)**. So, why not like that. If she has her leadership position there and also so to speak, "lives it out", or takes advantage of it, but at home is on a level with me, then that's completely okay."

Other interviewees, however, showed openness to equality or higher status of their partner in the profession even when personally affected. Here, according to Schwartz (2016), openness in relation to challenges in life can be identified.

> "**If your girlfriend was now in a leadership position, how would you like that?** That would be great, because she has just or she wishes to work in her parents' company and to take over the company someday. That means, she will also, when she takes over the company, she will maybe also become the boss. But that's the good question. She wishes to be a boss and to have her say here. It doesn't work out so well between the two of us. I wear the pants, but that will probably change over time. Then she will eventually "wear the pants". **And how would that be then?** Oh, if she wears the pants? Oh, that wouldn't be so great anymore. Because then it's again: "[Name of the interviewee, note of the authors], do this (...), do that (.), do this." But I actually cope with that quite well. Because I have to get along with her well. I have to accept her as she is. I have to accept her with her quirks and all. But yes, if she is the boss, then I will not say anything. Then she is just a boss. Then I have to eat humble pie. That's how it will be."

According to Schwarz (2016), it is evident here that some interviewees have the ability to observe, evaluate, deliberately reinforce their own behavior and flexibly align it with their own goals, also in relation to gender equality. This flexibility in thinking is particularly evident in one statement. The interviewee comments on the situation of women in working life, which is often worse than that of men, and tries to deal with the ideas of a biologization to explain behavioral differences between the sexes in a balanced way:

" I actually find that pretty shitty, because women are just like us, even if they are built more delicately, so to speak, not all are like that, many are different and if their way is blocked, so to speak, because someone who is above you does not accept it, then she can first, not prove herself, second, women, can also often be much tougher or prove themselves better than men, that they are the same, that they are better, that they get it done better, that they are smarter, just as they could be none of that but rather lower, so it is completely equal, it can be the same for both, that they are good in leadership positions, that they can lead the team well and so on. So it's actually complete bullshit, that the woman for example should stand in the kitchen, take care of it, because she earns less or because she, just because of this job and because she is simply a girl, a woman. That's just totally unnecessary and inhuman, because you exclude something, because you, because it's a woman."

Other interviewees question their own behavior or their own attitude towards the equality of women and men does not. A frequently cited explanation for the existing inequality between women and men in working life is the biological constitution of women, which does not enable them to receive equal pay for equal work. Here is an example of a young man who argues that men can take on more difficult work solely because of their physical constitution:

"Men are strong, I can say something like that too. Men are strong and they do difficult physical, yes, work. That's why women can't do that."

A conclusion that the interviewees themselves draw from their performances is that women, due to their physical constitution, earn less salary for their activities. A current survey by the Federal Statistical Office (Statistisches Bundesamt 2021) shows that women on average receive 19% less money per hour than men. The gender pay gap is therefore a reality in Germany, the reasons for this, however, are diverse. In particular, the traditional role distribution of the prevailing gender order leads to significantly more part-time work by mothers than fathers and fewer leadership positions (Hobler et al. 2017).

3.3 Self-Overcoming

Another dimension in Schwartz's (2016) value orientation is the "self-overcoming" of the individual in favor of societal structures. Self-overcoming implies universalism in that the individual has "understanding, appreciation, tolerance and protection of the well-being of all people and nature [in mind]" and can think and act autonomously (Bilsky 2015, p. 3). With regard to the present sample, there are indications of universalism, as among other things the Constitutional Law and other valid laws of the Federal Republic of Germany (e.g. the General Equal Treatment Act (AGG)) are considered by the interviewed interviewees as a starting point for interpersonal actions. The goodwill towards certain—sometimes disadvantaged—groups is another aspect to mention that is associated with self-overcoming.

The following statement by a young man about the equality of women and men in Germany shows that he regards the Constitutional Law as a starting point for interpersonal actions and classifies it as universally applicable law:

> "Of course, I find it very unfair in the first place, because, as you [the interviewer, note of the authors] already said, in principle every person is equal. We have had the Constitutional Law since 1949, in which all men and women are equal. [...] Everywhere women earn less. We have now strongly implemented in our company that we have women in leadership positions. So our women's quota is very high. We are also good at keeping up with that. But overall, of course, it is so that women are still not really in large leadership positions, earn less. It's just socially completely a no-go, in my opinion."

From the statement it becomes clear that the person interviewed regards the legal framework conditions of Article 3 Paragraph 2 of the Constitutional Law ("Men and women are equal. The state promotes the actual implementation of equality between women and men and works towards the elimination of existing disadvantages.") as a justification for an equality of women and men in Germany. However, he adds that the legal framework conditions do not correspond to reality and describes this as unacceptable. Another interviewee expresses a similar view, also stating that women and men should be treated equally, especially with regard to remuneration for work performance.

> "**How would you feel if more women were in leadership positions, so more women were bosses. At the moment, 80% of men are in a leadership position, they are the boss. How would it be if a bit more women were bosses? Do you think that's okay?** No, with that I have no problem. If the rules state that men and women should be equal, fifty-fifty bosses, then it must also be fifty-fifty in many things. Whether physical or something else. Women can also work properly, more than men. So women should actually also earn more than men."

3.4 Self-Enhancement

The last dimension of value orientation according to Schwartz (2016), standing in contrast to self-transcendence, is one's own "self-enhancement". This was emphasized by some interviewees especially in relation to their own individual mental and physical strength, their personal and professional performance and power or their own hedonism. The self-enhancement could also be demonstrated in relation to the topic of 'gender equality'. This is particularly evident in the following statement, in which the interviewee claims to have no problem with a professionally successful partner, but this is due to his desire for an intellectually equal partner. He justifies this desire with his own intellectual abilities.

> "**If your girlfriend were in a leadership position?** Higher than me in professional success? **Either higher or equal, definitely in a leadership position?** I would have absolutely no stress with that, because I say, personally it is important to me that in this case my girlfriend can intellectually offer at least as much as I can offer, I must be able to argue with my partner, it's pointless to have a dispute if you can't argue."

In some statements, the argument is also recognizable that biological differences justify a disadvantage in the payment of women. Structural political measures to support parents (e.g. through parental allowance) are unilaterally interpreted as an advantage for women and used as further justification for worse remuneration:

> "If, somehow, a woman works in construction, then it's clear, for me, that she earns less than a man.... A woman can just, let's say, not carry as much as a man. Or haul as much as a normal-. Of course there are also, I don't know so-. And women also get, what's it called, maternity leave or something. Or also here, if you have a child, then you also get, somehow, three years or so, paid vacation. **Yes, parental leave, that's what it's called. But a man could also take it.** Yes, yes. But it's more common with women. And it's clear that they earn less."

Other self-enhancing statements of the interviewed partners refer to a pronounced self-confidence. In the following statement, the egocentric worldview of a young man becomes clear, in which the needs of the potential partner do not play an explicit role, but she must have positive character traits:

> "A great character for me is, the woman must be open. The woman must accept my hobbies that I have. She must accept, that I don't always have time. She must also cope with the fact that I also write to other women. She must be nice. She must be friendly."

Another respondent also considers himself a "heteronormative standard model", without elaborating further. A questioning of what is considered "normally male" is not recognizable and the statement can be assessed as self-enhancement, as possibly other young men would have to compare themselves with him.

"So I think, I am kind of the heteronormative standard model. Exactly, a lot to do with boys, a lot to do with girls, had girlfriends and so on and so forth. Yes, I don't know, I feel too, normally male as a boy, I don't know."

4 Discussion

Refugee young men are accused by large parts of society of having a backward image of women and an anti-emancipatory attitude—this is explained and justified by the culture of the men in their countries of origin or their religious affiliation (Pfeiffer et al. 2018). The power of interpretation and above all the hierarchy of origin and gender in the associated debates is still held by a hegemonically dominant social group, which condemns the behavior of the refugee men and uses events such as the happenings of the Cologne New Year's Eve to distract from their own traditional gender image (AK FE.IN 2020; Mayer et al. 2016; Weidinger and Werner 2017). Groups of men with migration or refugee history are under general suspicion of viewing women as "objects". For this reason, it is necessary to deal with the issue of gender equality from a "post-migrant" perspective and to possibly dismantle existing ethno-sexist prejudices. For this, the named topics should be viewed from a societal perspective (Huxel et al. 2020). This not only includes a reflection of the "processes of inclusion and exclusion, of alienation and attribution", but also demands to "view racism and sexism as a problem of the entire society and as a part of negotiation processes with which societies react to the […] recognition of the fact of migration" (Huxel et al. 2020, p. 137).

With regard to the present study, it is clear that the young men of all three groups predominantly expressed themselves positively in relation to the equality of women and men. Here, the claim cannot be confirmed that young men with migration and refugee history consistently have an anti-emancipatory attitude. However, it can be shown that the attitudes of all surveyed young men are rather assigned to the traditional area.

This is particularly evident in the statements about ideas of relationships and partnership. Here, the preservation of a traditional family image (Oelkers 2012; Peuckert 2019) is predominantly in the foreground. In all three groups, a clear tradition of the "normal family image" with clearly assigned tasks (e.g., the mother takes care of the provision and education, the father provides the material basis for family life) was recognizable. An "idealized value order" in relation to a normal family image becomes clear (Beckers 2019, p. 509), which is also statistically reflected in the distribution of different family constellations in

Germany with 68.4% traditional family form (Statistisches Bundesamt 2018b). The fact that this traditional family form is accompanied by social inequalities is not least shown by the debate about the multiple burden on women during the Covid 19 pandemic, which was accompanied by a multitude of studies on the unfairly distributed care work between the genders (Hammerschmid et al. 2020; Kohlrausch and Zucco 2020). A broad discussion about values, family, gender, equality and not least care work is therefore necessary. Such a value discussion is shaped not only by societal and political debates, but also by legal norms (Beckers 2019). Therefore, for example, the introduction of "marriage for all" in 2017 is an important step towards an expanded perception of different life and family forms. A change or questioning of existing values is difficult for some of the surveyed young men, as their values reflect their own moral ideas and may have been shaped generationally by the family and peer group and were demonstrated to them.

Overall, it can be shown that the discussion about gender and equality is less a question of immigration or flight, but rather requires a societal debate in Germany.

References

Autor*innenkollektiv Fe.In. 2020. *Frauen*rechte und Frauen*hass: Antifeminismus und die Ethnisierung von Gewalt*. Berlin: Verbrecher Verlag.
BAMF (Bundesamt für Migration und Flüchtlinge). 2016. Bundesamt in Zahlen 2015. Asyl, Migration und Integration. http://www.bamf.de/SharedDocs/Anlagen/DE/Publikationen/Broschueren/bundesamt-in-zahlen-2015.pdf?__blob=publicationFile. Accessed: 9 July 2020.
Beckers, Tilo. 2019. Werte. In *Grundbegriffe der Soziologie*, ed. Johannes Kopp and Anja Steinbach, 507–511. Wiesbaden: Springer.
Becker-Schmidt, Regina. 1987. Die doppelte Vergesellschaftung – die doppelte Unterdrückung: Besonderheiten der Frauenforschung in den Sozialwissenschaften. In *Die andere Hälfte der Gesellschaft*. Eds. Lilo Unterkirchen and Ina Wagner, 10–25. Vienna: Österreichischer Soziologentag 1985.
Bilsky, Wolfgang. 2015. Psychologische Arbeiten zur Struktur menschlicher Werte. *Wissenswert* 8 (1): 5–12.
Bundeskriminalamt. 2019. Polizeiliche Kriminalstatistik. Bundesrepublik Deutschland Jahrbuch 2019, Vol. 4. Einzelne Straftaten/-gruppen und ausgewählte Formen der Kriminalität. https://www.bka.de/SharedDocs/Downloads/DE/Publikationen/PolizeilicheKriminalstatistik/2019/Jahrbuch/pks2019Jahrbuch4Einzelne.html. Accessed: 26 Jan 2021.
Bundeskriminalamt. 2020. Polizeiliche Kriminalstatistik. Bundesrepublik Deutschland. Jahrbuch 2019, Vol. 3, Tatverdächtige. Wiesbaden. https://www.bka.de/DE/AktuelleIn-

formationen/StatistikenLagebilder/PolizeilicheKriminalstatistik/PKS2019/PKSJahrbuch/pksJahrbuch_node.html . Accessed: 9 Febr 2021.

Bundesministerium für Familie, Senioren, Frauen und Jugend. 2017. *Engagement in der Flüchtlingshilfe*. Berlin. https://www.bmfsfj.de/bmfsfj/service/publikationen/engagement-in-der-fluechtlingshilfe/122012 . Accessed: 1 July 2020.

Degele, Nina. 2008. *Gender/Queer Studies*. Paderborn: Fink.

Dietze, Gabriele. 2016a. Das ‚Ereignis Köln'. *Femina Politica* 1: 93–102.

Dietze, Gabriele. 2016b. Ethnosexismus. Der Sex-Mob-Narrative um die Kölner Sylvesternacht. *movements* 2 (1): 1–16. http://movements-journal.org/issues/03.rassismus/10.dietze--ethnosexismus.html . Accessed: February 10, 2021.

Ege, Moritz, and Alexander Gallas. 2019. The exhaustion of merkelism: A conjunctual analysis. *New Formations* 96: 89–131. https://doi.org/10.3898/NEWF:96/97.04.2019.

Ehlert, Gudrun. 2012. *Gender in der Sozialen Arbeit*. Schwalenbach: Wochenschau Verlag.

Eickhorst, Andreas, and Katja Nowacki. 2019. Väterbilder – Die Rolle und Bedeutung der Väter in Familie und Jugendhilfe. In *Kindheit – vermessen und vergessen*. Eds. Bundesarbeitsgemeinschaft der Kinderschutz-Zentren e. V., 269–278. Köln: Bundesarbeitsgemeinschaft der Kinderschutz-Zentren e. V.

Elias, Norbert, and John L. Scotson. 2002. *Etablierte und Außenseiter*. Frankfurt/M: Suhrkamp.

Fachkommission der Bundesregierung zu den Rahmenbedingungen der Integrationsfähigkeit. 2020. Gemeinsam die Einwanderungsgesellschaft gestalten. Bericht der Fachkommission der Bundesregierung zu den Rahmenbedingungen der Integrationsfähigkeit. chrome-extension://efaidnbmnnnibpcajpcglclefindmkaj/https://www.fachkommission-integrationsfaehigkeit.de/resource/blob/1786706/1880170/917bc43f62136ed26ecef8125a4c9cdf/bericht-de-artikel-data.pdf?download=1. Accessed: September 1, 2024.

Grossmann, Karin, Klaus E. Grossmann, Elizabeth Fremmer-Bombik, Heinz Kindler, M. Hermann Scheuerer-Englisch, and Winter, and Peter Zimmermann. 2002. Väter und ihre Kinder – Die „andere" Bindung und ihre längsschnittliche Bedeutung für die Bindungsentwicklung, das Selbstvertrauen und die soziale Entwicklung des Kindes. In *Die Bedeutung des Vaters in der frühen Kindheit*, ed. Kornelia Steinhardt, Wilfried Datler, and Johannes Gstach, 43–72. Gießen: Psychosozial Verlag.

Hammerschmid, Anna, Julia Schmieder, and Katharina Wrohlich. 2020. Frauen in Corona-Krise stärker am Arbeitsmarkt betroffen als Männer. https://www.diw.de/documents/publikationen/73/diw_01.c.789749.de/diw_aktuell_42.pdf . Accessed: March 1, 2021.

Hark, Sabine, and Paula-Irene Villa. 2017. *Unterscheiden und herrschen. Ein Essay zu den ambivalenten Verflechtungen von Rassismus, Sexismus und Feminismus in der Gegenwart*. Bielefeld: transcript.

Hobler, Dietmar, Christina Klenner, Svenja Pfahl, Peter Sopp, and Alexandra Wagner. 2017. Wer leistet unbezahlte Arbeit? Hausarbeit, Kindererziehung und Pflege im Geschlechtervergleich, aktuelle Auswertungen aus dem WSI GenderDatenPortal, April 2017. https://www.boeckler.de/de/boeckler-impuls-unbezahlte-arbeit-frauen-leisten-mehr-3675.htm . Accessed: 26 Jan 2021.

Hurrelmann, Klaus, Gudrun Quenzel, Ulrich Schneekloth, Ingo Leven, Mathias Albert, Hilde Utzmann, and Sabine Wolfert. 2019. *Jugend 2019 – 18. Shell Jugendstudie*. Weinheim: Beltz.

Huxel, Katrin, Tina Spies, and Linda Supik. 2020. "PostKölnialismus" Otheringeffekte als Nachhall Kölns im akademischen Raum? In *Postmigrantisch gelesen. Transnationalität, Gender, Care*. Eds. Katrin Huxel, Juliane Karakayali, Ewa Palenga-Möllenbeck, Marianne Schmidbaur, Kyoko Shinozaki, Tina Spies, Linda Supik, and Elisabeth Tuider, 127–144. Bielefeld: transcript.

Kohlrausch, Bettina, and Aline Zucco. 2020. Die Corona-Krise trifft Frauen doppelt. https://www.boeckler.de/pdf/p_wsi_pb_40_2020.pdf . Accessed: 1 Mar 2021.

Kluckhohn, Clyde. 1951. Values and Value-Orientations in the Theory of Action: An Exploration in Definition and Classification. In *Toward a General Theory of Action*, ed. Talcott Parsons and Edward A. Shils, 388–433. Cambridge: Harvard University Press.

Mayer, Stefanie, Iztok Šori, and Birgit Sauer. 2016. Gendering 'the People'. Heteronormativity and 'Ethnomasochism' in Populist Imaginary. In *Populism, Media, and Education. Challenging Discrimination in Contemporary Digital Societies*. Ed. Maria Ranieri, 84–104. New York: Routledge.

Mayring, Philipp. 2015. *Qualitative Inhaltsanalyse: Grundlagen und Techniken*. Weinheim: Beltz.

Nowacki, Katja, Katja Sabisch, and Silke Remiorz. 2022. *Junge Männer in Deutschland*. Wiesbaden: Springer VS.

Oelkers, Nina. 2012. Familialismus oder die normative Zementierung der Normfamilie. Herausforderungen für die Kinder- und Jugendfamilie. In *Mutter + Vater = Eltern? Sozialer Wandel, Elternrollen und Soziale Arbeit*. Eds. Karin Böllert and Corinna Peter, 135–154. Wiesbaden: VS Verlag für Sozialwissenschaften.

Peuckert, Rüdiger. 2019. *Familienformen im sozialen Wandel*. Wiesbaden: Springer VS.

Pfeiffer, Christian, Dirk Baier, and Sören Kliem. 2018. Zur Entwicklung der Gewalt in Deutschland. Schwerpunkte: Jugendliche und Flüchtlinge als Täter und Opfer. Züricher Hochschule für Angewandte Wissenschaften. https://www.bmfsfj.de/blob/jump/121226/gutachten-zur-entwicklung-der-gewalt-in-deutschland-data.pdf . Accessed: 11 Febr 2021.

Pries, Ludger, ed. 2013. *Zusammenhalt durch Vielfalt? Bindungskräfte der Vergesellschaftung im 21. Jahrhundert*. Wiesbaden: Springer VS.

Pries, Ludger 2016. *Migration und Ankommen. Die Chancen der Flüchtlingsbewegung*. Frankfurt/New York: Campus.

Sanyal, Mithu M. 2017. PostKölnialismus. Feministischer Zwischenruf, Heinrich Böll Stiftung, Gunda Werner Institut, 25th January 25, 2017. https://www.gwi-boell.de/de/2017/01/25/postkoelnialismus. Accessed: 10 Febr 2021.

Schwartz, Shalom H. 1992. Universals in the content and structure of values: Theory and empirical tests in 20 countries. In *Advances in experimental social psychology*. Ed. Marc P. Zanna, 25: 1–65. New York: Academic Press.

Schmidt, Stefanie, Olivia Pettke, Robert J. B. Lehmann, and Klaus-Peter. Dahle. 2017. Sexualstraftäter ohne und mit Migrationshintergrund aus dem Nahen Osten und Nordafrika: Tatverhalten und Rückfallprognose. *Forensische Psychiatrie, Psychologische Kriminologie* 11 (5): 322–334. https://doi.org/10.1007/s11757-017-0441-4.

Schwartz, Shalom H. 2016. Basic individual values: Sources and consequences. In *Handbook of value: Perspectives from economics, neuroscience, philosophy, psychology and sociology*. Ed. Tobias Brosch and David Sander, 63–84. Oxford University Press.

Schwartz, Shalom H., and Wolfgang Bilsky. 1987. Toward a universal psychological structure of human values. *Journal of Personality and Social Psychology* 53: 550–562.

Statistisches Bundesamt. 2018a. Fachserie 1, Reihe 2.2 Bevölkerung und Erwerbstätigkeit, Bevölkerung mit Migrationshintergrund, Ergebnisse des Mikrozensus, Wiesbaden. https://www.destatis.de/DE/Themen/Gesellschaft-Umwelt/Bevoelkerung/Migration-Integration/Publikationen/Downloads-Migration/migrationshintergrund-2010220187004.pdf?__blob=publicationFile . Accessed: 8 Febr 2021.

Statistisches Bundesamt. 2018b. Familie, Lebensformen und Kinder. https://www.destatis.de/DE/Service/Statistik-Campus/Datenreport/Downloads/datenreport-2018-kap-2.pdf?__blob=publicationFile . Accessed: 11 Jan 2021.

Statistisches Bundesamt. 2021. Gender Pay Gap. https://www.destatis.de/DE/Themen/Arbeit/Arbeitsmarkt/Qualitaet-Arbeit/Dimension-1/gender-pay-gap.html . Accessed: 11 Jan 2021.

Thome, Helmut. 2019. Werte und Wertebildung aus soziologischer Sicht. In *Werte und Wertebildung aus interdisziplinärer Perspektive*, ed. Roland Verwiebe, 47–77. Wiesbaden: Springer VS.

Treibel, Annette. 2003. *Migration in modernen Gesellschaften. Soziale Folgen von Einwanderung, Gastarbeit und Flucht*. Weinheim/Munich: Beltz Juventa.

United Nations High Commissioner of Refugees (UNHCR). 2015. Abkommen über die Rechtsstellung der Flüchtlinge vom 28. Juli 1951. https://www.unhcr.org/dach/wpcontent/uploads/sites/27/2017/03/GFK_Pocket_2015_RZ_final_ansicht.pdf . Accessed: 9 Febr 2021.

VERBI Software. 2019. MAXQDA 2020 [computer software]. Berlin, Germany: VERBI Software. Available from maxqda.com.

Weidinger, Bernhard, and Katharina Werner. 2017. „Finger weg von unseren Frauen!" Männlichkeit, extreme Rechte und sexualisierte Gewalt. *Journal Für Psychologie* 25 (2): 153–178.

Werthschulte, Christian. 2017. „Nach" Köln ist wie „Vor" Köln. Die Silvesternacht und ihre Folgen. In *Köln*. Ed. APuZ, 10–17. Bonn.

Witzel, Andreas, and Herwig Reiter. 2012. *The problem-centred interview*. London: Sage.

Zick, Andreas, and Beate Küpper. 2015. Der Dreiklang aus Wut, Verachtung und Abwertung. In *Wut, Verachtung, Abwertung. Rechtspopulismus in Deutschland*. Eds. Ralf Melzer and Dietmar Molthagen, 11–14. Friedrich-Ebert-Stiftung. Bonn: Dietz.

Dr. Silke Remiorz *Department of Applied Social Sciences, University of Applied Sciences Dortmund*

Silke Remiorz received her degree and state recognition as a social pedagogue and social worker after studying social work at the University of Applied Sciences Dortmund in 2011. She then studied social sciences with a focus on "Restructuring of gender relations" at the Ruhr University Bochum, where she also received her doctorate in 2021. Since 2018, she has been a research assistant at the University of Applied Sciences Dortmund in the research project JUMEN (2018–2021). Her research foci include child and youth welfare and gender.

Prof. Dr. Katja Nowacki has been Professor of Clinical Psychology and Social Psychology at Dortmund University of Applied Sciences and Arts since 2007. Her research focuses on attachment and relationships, particularly in the context of child and family support, with a special focus on gender differences. In several research projects, she has looked at the influence of relationship experiences on boys and men, for example in a project on fathers with difficult family experiences. In the JUMEN research project, her primary interests are the influences of relationship experiences on attitudes towards gender and LGBTI. Prior to her academic work, she worked as a qualified social worker in the field of support for children, young people and their families.

Prof. Dr. Katja Sabisch *Section Gender Studies, Ruhr University Bochum*
Katja Sabisch studied sociology at the University of Bielefeld and has been a professor for Gender Studies at the Ruhr University Bochum since 2009. She primarily works on sociology of knowledge and history of gender inequality, family work and care, as well as methods of qualitative social research. She is the spokesperson of the Marie Jahoda Center for International Gender Studies at RUB and spokesperson of the Network Women's and Gender Research NRW.

"We've Gotten Used to the Headscarf!"

On Dealing with Cultural Diversity in a High-Rise Housing Estate in Hamburg

Astrid Wonneberger

1 Introduction

Dealing with diversity and cultural differences is part of everyday life for the approximately 3,000 residents of the Lenzsiedlung, a sociodemographically and culturally heterogeneous high-rise housing estate in the Hamburg district of Eimsbüttel. Over 70% of the residents have a migration background, originating in over 60 countries. Due to the high population density, the Lenzsiedlung is a well-suited setting for the investigation of perceptions, differences and changes regarding cultural values and norms that have been triggered or influenced by immigration to Germany.

Differences in attitudes, values, and norms[1] often become apparent in conflict situations. These include (in the context of this study) not only observable (physical or verbal) conflicts between actors, but also reflections on (everyday) situations that are perceived as problematic and that were, for example, discussed in conversations and guideline interviews by residents and professional actors. Hints of changes in attitudes, values, and norms can also be found in these statements, as this article will show.

---

[1] In this contribution, the terms "values", "norms", "attitudes" etc. are used with the same meaning as in the introduction to this anthology. A deeper discussion of the terms is therefore not necessary.

A. Wonneberger (✉)
Department Soziale Arbeit, HAW Hamburg, Hamburg, Germany
e-mail: astrid.wonneberger@haw-hamburg.de

© The Author(s), under exclusive license to Springer Fachmedien Wiesbaden GmbH, part of Springer Nature 2024
A. Wonneberger et al. (eds.), *Values and Value Change in the Post-Migrant Society*, https://doi.org/10.1007/978-3-658-45107-3_4

With this approach, I am following Max Gluckman's, Jaap van Velsen's and Clyde Mitchell's *Extended Case Method* or situational analysis (Gluckman 1961; van Velsen 1967; Mitchell 1983), in which small social events and everyday actions (or here: reflections) of individuals are analyzed in terms of how they interpret social values, rules, norms, and how they deal with them (cf. Rössler 2003, p. 144).

The following analyses are mostly based on 40 explorative and guideline interviews, which the POMIKU research team conducted with residents of the housing estate, users, and employees of the community center[2] during the first empirical phase of the project. These data are supplemented by seven interviews with people who, due to their professional activities in the district (e.g., in counselling centers, in a property letting agency, etc.), interact with residents of the Lenzsiedlung, and by data obtained through participant observation at various activities in the community center.

This contribution primarily focuses on a group of residents who are often overlooked in migration studies: "German-born"[3] residents in the housing estate and their attitudes towards the cultural diversity which they encounter every day. In this case, these are primarily senior residents, many of whom live in one of the two apartment blocks in the estate that are reserved for them. The research team was able to gain good access through the senior citizen work of the community center. In total, ten of the 40 exploratory interviews were conducted with senior residents between 60 and 93 years of age; I had further informal conversations on a trip for senior residents and at various events at the community center I took part in.

In a large high-rise housing estate such as the Lenzsiedlung, one would expect a broad range of neighborhood conflicts; and many such conflicts were addressed by the interviewees, both in interviews and in informal conversations. These included issues such as noise pollution from loud music or playing children,

---

[2] The community center of the Lenzsiedlung serves as a meeting place and venue for numerous activities for all residents in the housing estate and neighboring quarters. The services include counselling, open children's and youth work, recreational activities, communal events, and many more. The community center is run by the non-profit organisation Lenzsiedlung e. V., one of POMIKU's project partners.

[3] A discussion of the term "German" or "German culture" would go too far at this point. The quotation marks refer to the vague and fuzzy boundaries of this concept, which I am aware of. In this context, this term refers to people without a migratory background, as presently used by the Federal Statistical Office (Statistisches Bundesamt 2021).

incorrect waste disposal attracting rats, open alcohol consumption, harassment from smoke from a BBQ in the neighboring garden, or neighbors who would not say hello when passing by. However, all these conflicts, or annoyances, were not "culturalized" in the conversations I analyzed, i.e. associated with a certain cultural background. I therefore understand them as general problems of living close to each other that could occur in any neighborhood (cf. Althaus 2018, pp. 333–351). These "cases" (in the sense of the *Extended Case Method*) cannot be analyzed in connection with "cultural values", at least it is not apparent from our data whether individual or cultural behavior and preferences are assumed. Therefore, these topics will not be further dealt with.

However, there are also examples where cultural differences or corresponding attributions in relation to values and norms played an obvious role and were (at least partially) named as such. Three thematic areas have emerged as particularly significant:

Firstly, general attitudes towards migration influence the handling of cultural differences: What attitudes do people who encounter cultural diversity every day due to their living situation have towards immigration and cultural differences? Secondly, values and norms regarding religion, (foreign) religious practices, and increasing religious diversity are particularly frequently addressed. Especially Islam was discussed, which is not surprising, as it is a religion that is both different from the experiences of German-born seniors and currently being strongly discussed in our society. How do the interviewees perceive (foreign) religions? The third focus was "family", especially prompted by family-related questions as the major topic of our research project. What attitudes, values, and norms, especially in terms of gender and parenting, can be found here?[4]

Based on the analyses of interviews and observed case vignettes, selected situations of conflict and reflective statements will be analyzed in terms of underlying values and norms from these three thematic fields, guided by the following questions:

What are the (perceived) differences between residents of different origins regarding the above-mentioned selected values and norms (in terms of migration, religious diversity, family, parenting, and education)? Which values and norms are particularly often discussed, especially in the context of integration, participation, and inclusion? Why do these aspects seem to be particularly prone to conflict?

---

[4] See also the contribution by Stelzig/Weidtmann in this volume.

As the examples will show, attitudes (personal values) change in some cases through direct interaction. How open are (the interviewed) people living in the estate towards cultural diversity? Does this also indicate a value *change*? Is it adequate to speak of a "loss of values", which has been discussed since the 1970s (e.g. Noelle-Neumann 1978), or rather an increasing value plurality, as others proclaim (e.g. Terkessidis 2018, p. 110)?

And finally, the question arises whether these conflicts are about values at all or whether the differences should rather be analyzed at the level of norms and/ or behavior. Such a clarification may also provide new impulses for dealing with cultural differences to support and achieve a successful integration.

The selection of interviewees is not representative of the entire housing estate and certainly not for our society. We cannot draw any conclusions from our data about the frequency and distribution of such conflicts. Nevertheless, these individual cases show that certain attitudes exist, and they illustrate the heterogeneity of discussions and attitudes found in the Lenzsiedlung. From the analyses of the exemplary cases—tentatively and in combination with the findings of other studies on similar topics—generalizations can be made about the relationship between prejudices and tolerance. This, in turn, can lead to new insights about challenges and success factors for integration and participation in our society, from which implications for advisory and supporting institutions can be derived.

2 The Research Setting: The Lenzsiedlung

The Lenzsiedlung is situated in the district of Hamburg Eimsbüttel and was built as a social housing scheme between 1974 and 1984. Today, around 3,000 people are living in the high-rise housing estate in an area of 7.6 ha. The population density of 400 people per hectare (40,000 people per km^2) is one of the highest in Hamburg (Stadtteilbüro Lenzsiedlung 2007, p. 11).

The proportion of households with minor children is 29% (Hamburg: 18%), but single-person households are also frequent (42%), even though this rate is below the Hamburg average of 55%. 42% of these single-person households are over the age of 65 (Hamburg: 25%). Overall, there is a large variety of family and household forms, including above-average numbers of single parents and people receiving social welfare benefits (compared to Hamburg). Many residents have low educational and income levels; however, there are also inhabitants with higher educational degrees and well-paid jobs in the neighborhood. Over 70% of the residents have a migratory background. Today's cultural diversity of the

Lenzsiedlung is shaped by people from over 60 different countries (Statistikamt Nord 2018).

A wide discrepancy between internal and external perceptions of the neighborhood can be observed. Between the late 1980s and the early 2000s, the housing estate was characterized by major social problems and conflicts, which led to its reputation as a "no-go area". Various initiatives and actions, including a committed local civic work and a neighborhood development carried out from the year 2000 onwards were able to improve the quality of life and the image of the Lenzsiedlung significantly. Although the neighborhood still has the outdated reputation of a "social hotspot" (see Wonneberger et al. 2021 for details), most of the residents we talked to distance themselves from this image. Our interviewees repeatedly confirmed that they enjoy living in the housing estate. They feel safe and are overall satisfied with their living conditions.

3 Values, Norms, and Attitudes: Migration and Cultural Diversity

Studies on attitudes in the German population towards immigration and cultural diversity are numerous and agree on one point: individual attitudes vary greatly and range from complete rejection and negative attitudes to great tolerance and positive opinions. These attitudes are not solely determined by cultural and individual backgrounds, but apparently also largely depend on belonging to certain milieus (see Hradil 2018, pp. 23–32; Sinus Markt- und Sozialforschung 2016).

In a heterogeneous housing estate such as the Lenzsiedlung, a large variety of different attitudes towards migration and cultural diversity are to be expected. This will be confirmed later in this contribution. However, some of the interviewed German-born senior residents show some strikingly similar attitudes, as the following examples illustrate.

In the exploratory interviews, we asked, among other things, when and how the residents moved to the Lenzsiedlung and what their first impression was. Surprisingly often, the topics of immigration and cultural differences were brought up in response to this open question.[5] For example, an eighty-eight-year-old sen-

---

[5] The topic was addressed in five out of ten interviews. However, in two cases the question was omitted and in two other cases first-time residents were interviewed who had already moved into the housing estate at a time when there were hardly any foreign residents.

ior resident, who has lived in the Lenzsiedlung for seventeen years, responded as follows:

> "In the past, I never wanted to move here. When this was built [in the 1970s], we [she and her husband] lived across the street. And we knew that foreigners were moving in here. [...] We only drove by in the car at the time, and we said we would never move there. [...] Sometimes you say things and have no idea. [...] Then my husband died and I [...] got an offer here [for an apartment]. Where I never wanted to go. [...] And then I moved in here. [...] Since I've been living here, I'm the happiest person."[6]

This example is a typical statement of several interviewed senior residents who have moved into the housing estate in the last 20 years. They all had previously lived in very different living environments, had their own single-family home, or lived in large city apartments; some came from rural areas or wealthier neighborhoods such as Blankenese or Poppenbüttel. Like the eighty-eight-year-old senior resident quoted above, the others also emphasized that they would never have moved into a high-rise housing estate like the Lenzsiedlung before and only did so because they had no other choice. However, once they had moved in, they realized that life in the estate was much more pleasant than anticipated. On the contrary: they all currently expressed great satisfaction with their living situation.

As a reason for their original aversion to the neighborhood, the senior resident quoted above explicitly mentions "foreigners" and thus draws on a discourse that is still very popular and characterized by many stereotypical ideas. In other interviews, this derogatory image was supplemented by the also negatively connoted image of high-rise housing estates in general. The (conscious or unconscious) linking of different characteristics—in this case "foreigners" and "high-rise housing estates"—and their effects on individual residents and communities have been pointed out before by several studies (e.g. Yildiz 2015b; Ottersbach and Zitzmann 2009). How deeply these stereotypical images are anchored in our society is also shown by the fact that in this case (in retrospect) characteristics are mingled together that did not occur at the same time. As several first-time residents reported, only few "foreigners" lived in the neighborhood shortly after it was built in the 1970s (see also Gülay and Kuhn 2009). Accordingly, a seventy-year-old

---

[6] All interviews were conducted in German. The passages quoted in this article were translated by DEEPL and revised by the author for accuracy. The same applies for all statements quoted from sources originally published in German.

neighbor of the above-quoted resident, who has been living in the estate since the beginning and was present during the interview, commented her statement:

> "These are all prejudices! Life [in the neighborhood] is and was not that bad at all. [...] Those who caused trouble were not the foreigners, but Germans. [...] When the houses here were built, only people of German descent lived here."

He further explained that the housing estate had already become a "social hotspot" when hardly any "foreigners" lived there. Only when the settlement was no longer so attractive for "Germans", did immigrants move there in larger numbers.

Nevertheless, this negative stereotypical image of high-rise housing estates in combination with immigrants (or "foreigners") is very persistent, particularly in external perceptions of residents in neighboring quarters, as our research has also shown (see Wonneberger et al. 2021).

Conversations with senior residents also show that it is apparently personal experience and direct contacts with other residents that stimulate reflections and cause a change in attitude. For example, an eighty-nine-year-old interviewee explains:

> "What bothered me at the beginning, [...] here are many more foreigners [than in Blankenese]. And that was a bit frightening for me because I am not used to it. [...] But then I spoke with some of them. I do approach people. [...] And now I have to make friends with people who look foreign, but I have to deal with it because I live here. [...] And I think that people of my age should view migration a little differently. That one sees them primarily as people. And what they have experienced. I have experienced the war, I know what they have suffered. [...] You can learn this through conversations and open approach. [...] [My socialization] also shapes my image of this community here. I am prejudiced. But I am in the process of breaking it down. I say, they are people like you and me. [...] People can't help it that they grew up in Syria. They have a different language and culture, that's interesting. I am increasingly coming to this conclusion. A diversity. [...] It is a gain because by getting to know them you increase your self-awareness."

This example illustrates a change in attitude which takes place at an individual level. In this case, it was triggered by a direct (unavoidable) contact with people with a migratory background. In fact, we can find further examples for such a change in attitude in our study, as the following sections will show in more detail.

Of course, from these individual cases no statements about the overall societal prevalence of these attitudes and thus about a general change or even loss of values can be derived. Only when such processes of individual attitude change occur more frequently and spread, such attitudes can be understood as indicators of societal or cultural value change. In this context, cultural values and individual attitudes condition and influence each other: Shared attitudes create or influence cultural values. In this way, individuals can contribute to cultural change. At the same time, individual attitudes are also influenced by cultural values and norms in the context of socialization.[7]

A look at other studies helps to put these individual cases into a larger context:

For example, the German Institute for Economic Research (DIW) found in 2011 that Germans had generally become more open to immigration between 1996 and 2006, and the number of respondents with strong xenophobic attitudes had decreased, in West Germany from 9 to 4% and in East Germany from 15 to 4% (Diehl and Tucci 2011). The Robert Bosch Foundation also found in their "Diversity Barometer" a predominantly positive attitude towards diversity: According to their study, ethnic diversity is perceived more as an asset than as a danger (Robert Bosch Stiftung 2019). The ZuGleich study concludes that after a decline in the acceptance of diversity following the large waves of refugees in 2015, the survey value has returned to the 2014 level in 2020. 62.4% of the respondents answered that they were pleased about increasing diversity in Germany, while 20.4% rejected this (Zick and Krott 2021, p. 15). The ALLBUS Trend File 1980–2016 also notices a decrease in negative attitudes towards migration and assumes that immigration to Germany now seems to be accepted as a normality by the majority of the population (Fachkommission Integrationsfähigkeit 2020, pp. 54–55).

In the context of these findings, the attitudes observed in the Lenzsiedlung could be seen as further evidence of a change in values regarding immigration and cultural diversity. However, other studies come to a more critical conclusion:

According to the Leipzig Authoritarianism Study (LAS 2020), right-wing extremist (including xenophobic and Islamophobic) attitudes in Germany have been declining since 2020, but increases can also be observed regularly, triggered mainly by (perceived) societal crises. In addition, the study also notices a radicalization, especially among young people, and a polarization of society, especially

---

[7] I am referring here to an ethnological concept of culture which assumes that culture is supra-individual, i.e. shared by many people. As part of culture, values and norms are also shared. People learn culture through the process of socialization and thus, consciously, or unconsciously, adopt many of the prevalent values and norms. At the same time, people can learn different cultural traits throughout their lives. They can choose values, norms, or patterns of behavior situationally or modify them and thus contribute to a change in values (see in detail Beer 2017, pp. 73–80).

between East and West Germany. Therefore, there is "no room for complacency" (LAS 2020, pp. 79–83). The ZuGleich study also observes an increase in xenophobia, especially towards Muslims, compared to 2014 (Zick and Krott 2021, pp. 24–27).

A change in values (as opposed to attitudes) can only be cautiously assumed. However, the data from the Lenzsiedlung can be seen as further evidence for Gordon Allport's well-tested contact hypothesis (1954). This hypothesis states that individual prejudices can be reduced through direct contact (cf. Brown and Hewstone 2005; Pettigrew and Tropp 2006). This correlation is also assumed by the Leipzig Authoritarianism Study as a partial explanation for the differences between East and West Germany (LAS 2020, p. 48). In our case of the Lenzsiedlung, at least individual residents are encouraged to engage with increasing cultural diversity and to reflect on the value of "tolerance" by daily and direct encounters, in the elevators, the courtyard, or the local community center.

Another situation illustrates this point: when the topics "residents of Turkish descent" and "Islam" were discussed in a round table in the local community center, an over eighty-year-old participant asked several times whether the term "Turkish" should be used at all or whether it was a discriminatory term. At the same time, she did not know an alternative term. The fact that she asked this question points at a reflective approach to differences, in this case to using a politically correct language for people with a migratory background. This uncertainty about politically correct norms (in terms of language) reveals the underlying value of tolerance and the desire not to discriminate against anyone, not even through potentially derogatory terms.

Of course, the neighborhood is not a homogeneous community, and not all interviewees expressed themselves so positively, openly, and reflectively towards us. It is to be assumed that it was particularly open-minded people who made themselves available to us as interviewees. Every now and again, we also witnessed more xenophobic statements. In one case, for instance, a resident explicitly stated that there were "too many foreigners" living in the housing estate, and we also heard of AfD-voters who expressed similar attitudes. Moreover, it is likely that tenants who were dissatisfied with their living situation would have moved out of the estate as soon as possible, and therefore we would not have met them. Nevertheless, these individual cases show that at least some residents reflect on their images of and attitudes towards migration and high-rise housing estates, especially when they are prompted to do so through direct contacts. Tolerance (in the sense of acceptance of cultural differences) is an important shared value, which was also explicitly named as such by residents with a migratory background. This becomes particularly visible in reflection processes, as the interview statements illustrate. However, tolerance also has limits, especially when it comes to religious diversity.

4   Values, Norms, and Attitudes: Religious Diversity

The "Diversity Barometer" of the Robert Bosch Foundation (2019) shows that of all the dimensions surveyed (including disability, gender, sexual orientation, ethnic origin) religious diversity has the lowest level of acceptance among the respondents. This result points at a great divide in the German population. Opinions range from acceptance to complete rejection of non-Christian religious expressions and symbols in Germany (Robert Bosch Stiftung 2019, pp. 12, 36–38). Other studies come to a similar conclusion, finding that religious diversity is seen both as a cultural asset and as a cause of conflict. These attitudes can be found in all regions of Germany in roughly equal distribution (Klinkhammer and Neumaier 2020, p. 9; cf. also Pollack and Müller 2013, p. 36). Which of these attitudes towards which aspects of religious diversity can be found in the Lenzsiedlung? How is religious diversity experienced and evaluated here?

Religious diversity was often discussed in the context of reflections on cultural diversity in the neighborhood. The following attitudes are particularly interesting, as they were expressed by several interviewees independently of each other:

> "Last week there was one woman [in the courtyard] who was completely veiled, that's not my thing. It also scares me, I must honestly say. You don't know what's behind it. [...] But otherwise—I mean, you've gotten used to the headscarf. [...] And that doesn't really bother me anymore." (75-year-old resident)
>
> "There are also many women living in this house with headscarves etc. I don't find that so bad anymore today. [...] I don't think the burka is okay, though, legally. Completely veiled they can do anything; you don't know who you're dealing with. I don't understand how German women who convert to Islam can go along with this." (89-year-old resident)
>
> "There is the religion [Islam], as normal people live it. I'm not bothered by the headscarves either, others are bothered by the headscarves, I'm not, they can wear their headscarves, I don't mind. The ordinary religious people, [they don't bother me], but then there is the more extreme side of Islam. [...] [I once talked to a Muslim], he had a very callous attitude that everyone ultimately must pray to Allah, and that's not possible. That's an extreme." (72-year-old resident)

As in the previous section, the first two statements reveal a change in personal attitudes and possibly also a change in cultural values in terms of religious norms and practices, which is particularly manifested in the confrontation with the headscarf. In the past, these two residents were rather critical towards Islam and the headscarf, but now they have become used to it. Even if this is not a positive perception, it is at least a neutral attitude. And the third example also demonstrates that the headscarf and "normal" Islam (whatever that means exactly) are generally accepted, which indicates a growing tolerance towards religious diversity. But there is a clear limit to what is perceived as "good" or "neutral" and thus tolerated: full veiling and "extreme" Islam (and the values and norms associated with it) are not acceptable, at least not in the perceptions of the interviewees. Another senior resident went even further and explicitly demanded in an informal discussion round:

> "You see so many fully veiled women here. We are not in Turkey! If you live here, you have to adapt!"

These attitudes coincide with the results of other studies on this topic: Basically, a large part of the German population (87% of West Germans, 78% of East Germans) believe that one should be open to any religion. At the same time, however, the increasing diversity of religious groups is perceived as a cultural asset by significantly fewer people (61% of West Germans and 57% of East Germans). About two-thirds of the German population regard the increasing diversity of religious groups as a cause of conflict (Klinkhammer and Neumaier 2020, p. 24; cf. Pollack and Müller 2013, pp. 35–36). Pollack and Müller interpret this as a "high problem and reality awareness of the German population", which does not block itself off to positive aspects of religious diversity, but remains critical (Pollack and Müller 2013, p. 36; cf. also Klinkhammer and Neumaier 2020, p. 22).

Compared to other religions, Islam is viewed particularly critically by most Germans: Less than a third of West Germans (31%) and a quarter of East Germans (21%) see Islam as an asset, and 49% of West Germans and 57% of East Germans even perceive it as a threat (Klinkhammer and Neumaier 2020, pp. 24–25; cf. also Frindte et al. 2011, pp. 16–17, 21). The ZuGleich study found a Muslim hostility of 34.2% in its 2020 survey (Zick and Krott 2021, p. 27). The statements of the three residents quoted above also imply this threat, but they distinguish between different types of Islam and thus demonstrate a more differentiated view than perceiving all Muslims collectively as a threat.

The interviewees' statements about the headscarf and full veiling are embedded in a "headscarf dispute" which has been prominent in Germany since the 1990s (see in detail e.g. Berghahn and Rostock 2009; bpb 2005; Korteweg and Yurdakul 2016; Amir-Moazami 2007). This debate has not lost any of its significance up to date. As the first two statements also show, this concern is only ostensibly about the headscarf as a religiously justified dress code, the symbolic value is rather multifaceted and complex. What is actually being negotiated is the importance of religion in an ideologically neutral state, assumed differences between one's own and foreign cultures, and self-perceptions and perceptions of others. Islam and the headscarf as its symbol often become representative for perceived threats to Western values such as gender equality or security. According to a survey by Klinkhammer and Neumaier (2020), many Germans associate Islam in general and the headscarf in particular with negative characteristics, such as the oppression of women (82% of West Germans, 81% of East Germans), fanaticism (73% in the West, 71% in the East), propensity for violence (61% in the West, 67% in the East), and narrow-mindedness (53% each) (similarly also Frindte et al. 2011, pp. 16–17). Positive connotations such as peacefulness, tolerance, respect for human rights, and solidarity are only associated with Islam by five percent of the West and nine percent of the East German respondents (Klinkhammer and Neumaier 2020, p. 24).

The residents of the Lenzsiedlung also locate themselves within this discourse, when they express their concerns about full veiling for security reasons, or when they interpret certain, strangely appearing behaviors as a violation against equality, as the following statement by a 75-year-old resident illustrates:

> "I really notice that foreign men don't look at you. When they meet me, they look down. As if one is inferior, that's my feeling. I don't think that's right. […] [In another block] there is also one resident who was involved in the mosque here, […] he also had that look about him. That you as a woman have to—[…] I don't think that's right."

These values also receive such great attention because they are fundamental values with corresponding norms, where compliance is very strictly expected. Violations against these values and norms, such as equality, security etc.—even if there are only concerns that such violations might occur—immediately provoke outrage (Hradil 2018, p. 31). Lingen-Ali and Mecheril (2020) point out that confrontations with modern gender norms and values are particularly emotionally charged. This also became evident in the last example from the Lenzsiedlung.

Religious differences remain a potential source of conflict, especially Islam (Klinkhammer and Neumaier 2020, p. 24). However, not all these conflicts are based on skepticism or intolerance. In some cases, different behavioral norms which do not seem to be compatible with indigenous norms might cause conflicts: Apparently, "disputes" about noise disturbances in the Lenzsiedlung happen frequently. Particularly, when Muslim families get together after dark "for eating, cooking and laughing" to celebrate Ramadan, while their non-Muslim neighbors would like to spend a quiet evening, conflicts arise, as an employee of a local housing company reported.

However, we also encountered a great openness and interest towards Islam with many interviewees. For example, when a young Muslim woman took part in the "storytelling café", which took place several times a year in the community center,[8] the conversation spontaneously shifted from the original topic to Islam, and the Muslim woman quickly found herself in the role of the interviewee. The atmosphere among the attending senior women was overall very open and interested. This again points to the importance of Allport's contact hypothesis, and Klinkhammer and Neumaier (2020, p. 25) also note: In areas, in which only few contacts between the non-Muslim and Muslim population exist, the attitude towards Islam is more negative and rejecting. Intercultural places of interaction and meeting points are therefore of major importance.

5 Values, Norms, and Attitudes: Family and Parenting

Cultural diversity concerning family forms and family-related behavioral norms are a central part of societal discourses on immigration and integration. Numerous studies on these topics deal with attitudes, values, and norms in relation to family (e.g. BMFSFJ 2010, 2020; Sinus Milieustudien; Family reports of the federal government). This includes the research projects in the BMBF funding line "migration and societal change", some of which are presented here. The concept of family and the idea of a "good family" also repeatedly emerged in the research conducted in the Lenzsiedlung, not only, but particularly among the senior residents who are the focus here.

Before analyzing individual cases of cultural diversity, I would like to start this section by pointing out some cultural universals:

There is no (known) society without families, even though the specific form can vary greatly between cultures (see Ember and Ember 2015, p. 252). It can probably be claimed with some certainty (even though this is difficult to

---

[8] The "Erzählcafe" (storytelling café) is a social event in the community center of the Lenzsiedlung, which has been developed and tested as part of the joint project POMIKU. It invites residents from the surrounding neighborhoods to chat and discuss a loosely defined topic over coffee and cake, thus promoting intercultural communication.

empirically verify) that family, children, and familial cohesion are among the most important cultural basic values in all societies.

Statements by people who value family (as a cultural institution, not necessarily as an individual attitude in individual cases) and its important functions can also be found in the Lenzsiedlung. Positive characteristics and connotations of "family" were mentioned by residents of different age groups and with various cultural backgrounds.[9] For example, a 30-year-old resident with Armenian background states, "family is very important and takes up the most space", and for a 16-year-old teenager with Kurdish background, family is "showing love and loyalty". Two 15- and 17-year-old residents with Turkish background describe family as "the people you can be open with, who stand behind you and always help. You are there for each other. Family is not only there when you need them." For a 14-year-old resident with Ghanaian background, family consists of "your closest people who take care of you and solve all your problems when you need help and with whom you can always talk". A 33-year-old resident with Kurdish background resumes:

> "Being together as a family, being there for each other, feeling love, giving love, that's important. [...] Family also means there is a place to retreat. [...] These are the roots, stability, when I give my children the roots and strength and when I am there for them. Then they also develop a strong self-confidence. [...] I know, my parents are there for me, and then family gains its own strength. Family, being there for each other, being together, having things in common [...] Family is everything, it is very important. [...] [The family is] there for me."

And a 70-year-old senior without migratory background states:

> "The family is always the most important thing. I do have many friends [...], but the family is [...] always the most important thing, no matter what. Family always comes first."

These examples could easily be continued.

Family is apparently a widely shared and common basic value. However, the specific (behavioral) norms, how it should be designed and structured, what a family should be like and what not, what makes a "good" family and how one should behave so that family and society function best, cannot only vary indi-

---

[9] See also Bührig and Mittag (2023) in the German version of this volume.

vidually, but also globally between cultures and societies (for overviews see e.g. Ember and Ember 2015; Haviland et al. 2011).

Just like family, children are also a universal value, and in all cultures, parents strive to give their children a successful start in life and do everything to ensure their well-being and good future. But how these goals can best be achieved, how parenting, socialization, and education practices should be designed etc., are questions that are not only answered differently by individuals, but also reflect cultural differences. Such underlying shared belief systems, so-called "parental theories" or "parental ethnotheories" (Ember and Ember 2015, p. 59; Harkness et al. 2009), can lead to conflicts (see e.g. Ember and Ember 2015, pp. 57–69; Arnett and Maynard 2013).

During our research in the Lenzsiedlung, we came across several ethnotheories in various situations, including attitudes towards different aspects of parenting, family, education, child development, socialization etc.

In one interview situation, the topic of the "correct" or "best" way to raise children was addressed. At the "breakfast with an interesting guest"[10] a resident told me about her experiences with refugee families with whom she had worked voluntarily for a long time:

> "What particularly bothered me is that the parents do not play with the children at all. It is important that parents play with their children!"

This statement expresses the Western cultural belief that parents playing with their children is an important part of good upbringing and socialization. Parents who do not do this are accordingly viewed critically (Ember and Ember 2015, pp. 59–62).

In this case, these different behavioral norms can be explained by cultural differences (even if the exact cultural backgrounds cannot be traced back in this case). Outside of Western cultures, playing between adults and children is rather unusual. However, this does not mean that children do not play at all. Instead, they either play alone, make their own toys, or play with peers (Ember and Ember 2015, p. 62; Arnett and Maynard 2013, p. 281; LeVine and New 2008; Lancy 2008, pp. 224–228).

---

[10] The "Frühstück mit interessantem Gast" is a monthly event at the community center, where invited guest speakers give a presentation on a current and/or entertaining topic while the listeners are having breakfast. The event is particularly popular with seniors.

The fact that families with a migratory background are expected to adjust in various respects is also evident in the example of another senior resident who emphasizes that the newcomers must make an effort to learn the German language and to adapt to German educational norms. In her opinion, this is best to be achieved through direct contact with German families instead of isolation, which has often been observed in the past, especially after family reunification. What makes this case special is that this woman does not only express her expectations and demands, but she also helps to implement them. Together with another senior resident, she is a "godmother-grandma" for a family with a Kurdish background in the Lenzsiedlung. She sees the goal of this godparenthood in the fact that this family can "get to know the German culture [better], because their children live here in Germany". While, in her opinion, it is good to preserve some cultural norms, there are many German customs and traditions that are taken for granted by the German population, but which families with a migratory background have still to learn. This includes language skills and especially how to play with the children, which she conveys in regular meetings with the family. This works not only because the family and the godmother-grandmas liked each from the start, but above all because the family are open to "new" norms, such as playing with children. This godmotherhood has developed so well that both sides now see themselves as "one family", and the family with Kurdish background is "totally integrated". In this case, the interviewee understands integration primarily as the (Kurdish) family's adaptation to the values and norms applicable in Germany regarding child rearing. However, she also adds in the interview that integration must take place from both sides and that she has also learned a lot from the family's culture, especially a greater "sense of family" than she sees in "the German culture".

In the case of this godmother relationship, or socialization partnership, as it might also be called, many factors on both sides seem to support this success, including openness, sympathy, interest in children, time, etc., but also the willingness (here especially on part of the family of Kurdish descent) to get to know and adopt "foreign" values and norms. Thus, this relationship has existed for so long and—this is the godmother-grandma's conclusion—has also promoted integration.[11]

---

[11] In my research, I have so far only found one other project that was similarly designed: In the Austrian "Grandma/Grandpa Project" in 2011, seniors offered learning aid to pupils with a migratory background. The major aim of this project was to improve integration and participation opportunities (Association NL 40 2011; Znidar 2011).

The vignettes also show that the question of "good" parenting, socialization, child development, and education is considered so important that adaptation efforts on the part of families with migration experiences are expected, at least at the level of norms and behavior, even if a change in values does not necessarily seem necessary.

The belief that it is generally appropriate to expect a (one-sided) adaptation effort from immigrants (i.e. assimilation), is rather popular. According to the ZuGleich study 2020, 31% of respondents favor a form of assimilation which includes participation in our society. Another 10.5% demand assimilation, but at the same time reject social participation. Only just under 48% are convinced that integration is the ideal solution to deal with cultural differences. Integration in this context means that adjustments need to be made on all sides, that the exchange process is mutual, that the maintenance of cultural characteristics and identities is accepted, while social participation is also granted (Zick and Krott 2021, pp. 7–10).

6 Conclusion

What can be concluded from these examples? What findings can be derived from these conflict "cases" and reflections about values, norms, behavior, and cultural change?

Some of the presented vignettes indicate individual changes in attitude towards an image of our society—resp. high-rise housing estates—which is characterized by an increasing diversity due to migration. In the cases presented here, these transformation processes are mainly triggered by direct encounters with cultural diversity: by living together or close to each other, meeting people with different cultural backgrounds in small talk situations or even getting to know them better in community events. This can lead to new perspectives and help to reduce existing reservations. From a post-migrant perspective (see e.g. Yildiz and Hill 2015; Fouroutan et al. 2018), one could also put it this way: Residents are increasingly acknowledging migration as a fact, but do not yet take diversity for granted, as some aspects are still too "foreign" to them. However, direct encounters leads to an increased reflection on one's own attitudes and behaviors, even if not all "foreign" values and norms are accepted without criticism. It is the boundaries that are rather reflected upon: What do I perceive positively? Which aspects do I not care about, so I rate them neutrally? What can I tolerate? What can I not accept? This questioning and exploring of new value boundaries can also be seen as a step towards dissolving the established, dichotomous view of "native normality and immigrant problems", as Yildiz 2015a (p. 22) named it.

Against the background of politically and socially desired integration, not all differences are discussed equally, as was also shown in the interviews. Aspects that have long been fought for in our society and do not yet seem to be fully achieved seem particularly prone to conflict and are often emotionally charged, as many people are afraid that these achievements could be lost again. This applies especially to relatively "new" basic values such as gender equality or a "modern" form of parenting and education, where the effects could be particularly bad if values and norms changed into a "wrong", because "backward", direction (cf. Lingen-Ali and Mecheril 2020). In this context, expectations regarding adjustments are uttered more frequently than in other cases.

In some cases, stereotypical attributions and ideas also seem to play a role when "foreign" cultures are evaluated. For example, some statements by the residents of the Lenzsiedlung indicate that Islam is frequently associated with gender hierarchies, backwardness, and potential danger (keyword: terrorism), an observation which Klinkhammer and Neumaier (2020, pp. 24–27, 133–144, 177) have also made. What is often missing is a more differentiated view, which should be based on a greater knowledge of cultural backgrounds and the complexity of Islam. Such deeper knowledge would be of great importance for future coexistence and cohesion.

Some general conclusions can be derived from these findings for professional practice: Firstly, the importance of specific meeting places, where people of different backgrounds can get to know each other, and spaces for intercultural encounters, where values and behavioral norms can be mutually conveyed and discussed, cannot be overemphasized. Institutions of interreligious dialogue (Klinkhammer and Neumaier 2020, p. 49 ff.) and community centers with open and easily accessible meeting points and events are as important as an inviting design of courtyards, entrance areas, corridors, and well-maintained playgrounds in housing estates. At this point, urban planning, housing agencies, and housing cooperatives are also responsible for counteracting the emergence of ethnic enclaves and promoting social cohesion through their policies and actions (see in detail e.g. Schnur et al. 2013; Baumgärtner 2013; Müller 2013; Althaus 2018, p. 353 ff.). Meeting places are not only important for migrants, as other publications have also pointed out (e.g. IHS 2017, pp. 38–49), but for all residents, regardless of how long they have been living in the neighborhood.

Secondly, individual adaptation efforts and reflections on one's own attitudes and images are also required, and this applies to all residents, including those who consider themselves native, and to professional players alike. Often, an open general attitude may be a good start, such as showing interest to learn more about Islam through a conversation with a Muslim woman, which might lead to a changed perspective. The question arises how such openness can be further promoted. Support from professional players and stakeholders such as local community centers again play an important role by enabling contacts and providing spaces for encounters in various settings. In other cases, it may be useful to initiate exchange relationships or, where they already exist, to further intensify them, as the example of godmotherhoods has illustrated. It is important in all these settings to have a balanced exchange, without one-sided, predetermined expectations or prejudices. Such implementations can directly or indirectly promote openness and at least contribute to a change in attitude, for all individual actors. Ultimately, this might lead to a long-term change in values and to a greater accepted range of cultural diversity itself, without endangering established and reliable basic values.

At this point, it should also be noted that not all social debates in which "values" are disputed or perceived as threatened are about values. In many cases, it is rather behavioral norms or the actual behavior of individuals which is criticized, generalized, and culturalized without deeper reflection. The basic values of our society are shared and accepted by most of the population, regardless of their cultural background. Many studies have shown this (e.g. BMFSFJ 2010, p. 16; Uslucan 2013, pp. 238–239). Freedom, security, tolerance, freedom of religion, family and family support, education, good parenting, and favorable conditions for raising children—these are basic values which the vast majority of our society agree upon (see e.g. IfD Allensbach 2020; Values Index 2020; Encyclopedia of Value Perceptions 2020; Klinkhammer and Neumaier 2020). Recent incidents and studies might point to a growing number of people who reject some of these basic values, including gender equality; however, there is evidence that many of those are people of German descent. There is no clear boundary between people with and without a migratory background or different cultural groups in terms of attitudes towards basic values.

This also means that a (repeatedly discussed and partially demanded) change of values (at a cultural level) is often not necessary for people with a migration background. However, the different (individual and culturally shaped) perspectives on which behavioral norms are acceptable and which are not, can lead to conflicts. This may be another starting point for professional practice, as has already been pointed out (e.g. IHS 2017, p. 29, 34): It can be helpful in conversations and encounter situations to use the existing similarities as a basis for communication, instead of focusing on differences. Reflections on shared values can then help to view and discuss normative differences more openly and in a differentiated way, which will ultimately help to strengthen and sustain social cohesion.

References

Allport, Gordon W. 1954. *The Nature of Prejudice*. Reading: Addison-Wesley.
Althaus, Eveline. 2018. *Sozialraum Hochhaus. Nachbarschaft und Wohnalltag in Schweizer Großbauten*. Bielefeld: transcript.
Amir-Moazami, Schirin. 2007. *Politisierte Religion. Der Kopftuchstreit in Deutschland und Frankreich*. Bielefeld: transcript.
Arnett, Jeffey Jensen, and Ashley E. Maynard. 2013. *Child Development. A Cultural Approach*. Boston: Pearson.
Baumgärtner, Esther. 2013. Scapegoating, stakeholding and gatekeeping: Techniken der Inklusion und Exklusion in heterogenen Stadtquartieren. In *Migrationsort Quartier. Zwischen Segregation, Integration und Interkultur*. ed. Olaf Schnur, Philipp Zakrzewski, and Matthias Drilling, 121–134. Wiesbaden: Springer VS.
Beer, Bettina. 2017. Kultur und Ethnizität. In *Ethnologie. Einführung in die Erforschung kultureller Vielfalt*, eds. Bettina Beer, Hans Fischer, and Julia Pauli, 71–88. 9th ed., Berlin: Reimer.
Berghahn, Sabine, and Petra Rostock, eds. 2009. *Der Stoff, aus dem Konflikte sind. Debatten um das Kopftuch in Deutschland, Österreich und der Schweiz*. Bielefeld: transcript.
BMFSFJ (Federal Ministry for Family Affairs, Senior Citizens, Women and Youth). 2010. Ehe, Familie, Werte – Migrantinnen und Migranten in Deutschland. Monitor Familienforschung. Beiträge aus Forschung, Statistik und Familienpolitik, Issue 24. https://www.bmfsfj.de/newsletter/bmfsfj/themen/familie/76214?view=DEFAULT. Accessed 24 June 2021.
BMFSFJ (Federal Ministry for Family Affairs, Senior Citizens, Women and Youth). 2020. Gelebte Vielfalt: Familien mit Migrationshintergrund in Deutschland. Berlin. https://www.bmfsfj.de/blob/116880/a75bd78c678436499c1afa0e718c1719/gelebte-vielfalt--familien-mit-migrationshintergrund-in-deutschland-data.pdf. Accessed 24 June 2021.
Bpb (Bundeszentrale für politische Bildung/Federal Agency for Civic Education). 2005. Debatte Konfliktstoff Kopftuch. http://creativecommons.org/licenses/by-nc-nd/3.0/de/. Accessed 24 June 2021.
Brown, Rupert, and Miles Hewstone. 2005. An Integrative Theory of Intergroup Contact. *Advances in Experimental Social Psychology* 37: 255–343.
Bührig, Kristin, and Romy Mittag (2023) Werte und Bewertungsverfahren von Jugendlichen im postmigrantischen Kontext. Exemplarische Analyse zum Positionieren im Interview. In *Werte und Wertewandel in der postmigrantischen Gesellschaft*, eds. Astrid Wonneberger, Sabina Stelzig, Katja Weidtmann, and Diana Lölsdorf, 187–211. Wiesbaden: Springer VS.
Diehl, Claudia, and Ingrid Tucci. 2011. Fremdenfeindlichkeit und Einstellungen zur Einbürgerung. *DIW Wochenbericht* Nr. 31 „Wer darf Deutsche/r werden?", 3–8.
Ember, Carol R., and Melvin Ember. 2015. *Cultural Anthropology*. Boston: Pearson.
Enzyklopädie der Wertvorstellungen. 2020. Ranking der Werte (January 2014–March 2020). https://www.wertesysteme.de/werte-ranking/. Accessed 24 June 2021.
Fachkommission Integrationsfähigkeit. 2020. Gemeinsam die Einwanderungsgesellschaft gestalten. Bericht der Fachkommission der Bundesregierung zu den Rahmenbedingungen der Integrationsfähigkeit. https://www.fachkommission-integrationsfähigkeit.de/

resource/blob/1786706/1787474/fb4dee12f1f2ea5ce3e68517f7554b7f/bericht-de-data.pdf?download=1. Accessed 14 Dec 2021.

Frindte, Wolfgang, Klaus Boehnke, Henry Kreikenbom, and Wolfgang Wagner. 2011. Lebenswelten junger Muslime in Deutschland. Ein sozial- und medienwissenschaftliches System zur Analyse, Bewertung und Prävention islamistischer Radikalisierungsprozesse junger Menschen in Deutschland. Abschlussbericht (final report),published by the Bundesministerium des Innern, Berlin. https://www.researchgate.net/publication/308914880_Lebenswelten_junger_Muslime_in_Deutschland_Ein_sozial-_und_medienwissenschaftliches_System_zur_Analyse_Bewertung_und_Pravention_islamistischer_Radikalisierungsprozesse_junger_Menschen_in_Deutschland#fullTextFileContent. Accessed 24 June 2021.

Fouroutan, Naika, Juliane Karakayali, and Riem Spielhaus, eds. 2018. *Postmigrantische Perspektiven*. Bonn: bpb.

Gluckman, Max. 1961. Ethnographic Data in British Social Anthropology. *Sociological Review* 9 (1): 5–17.

Gülay, Cem, and Helmut Kuhn. 2009. *Türken-Sam. Eine deutsche Gangsterkarriere*. Deutscher Taschenbuchverlag: Munich.

Harkness, Sara, Charles M. Super, Moisés Ríos. Bermúdez, Ughetta Moscardino, Marjolijn Blom, Jong-Hay. Rha, Caroline Johnston Mavridis, Sabrina Bonichini, Blanca Huitrón, Barbara Welles-Nyström, Jesús Palacios, On-Kang Hyun, Grace Soriano, and Piotr Olaf Zylicz. 2009. Parental Ethnotheories of Children's Learning. In *The Anthropology of Learning in Childhood*, eds. David F. Lancy, John Bock, and Suzanne Gaskins, 65–81. Lanham: AltaMira Press.

Haviland, William A., Harald E.L. Prins, Bunny McBride, and Dana Walrath. 2011. *Cultural Anthropology*. The Human Challenge. 13th ed. Wadsworth, International Edition.

Hradil, Stefan. 2018. Der Wert von Werten: Wozu sind sie gut und wie entstehen sie? In *Werte – Und was sie uns wert sind. Eine interdisziplinäre Anthologie*. eds. Randolf Rodenstock and Neşe Sevsay-Tegethoff, 19–36. Munich: Roman Herzog Institut e. V.

IfD Allensbach. 2020. Allensbacher Markt- und Werbeträger-Analyse – AWA 2020. Statista 2021. https://de.statista.com/statistik/daten/studie/170820/umfrage/als-besonders-wichtig-erachtete-aspekte-im-leben/. Accessed 24 June 2021.

IHS Zentrum für globale Fragen an der Hochschule für Philosophie. 2017. Gelingende Wertebildung im Kontext von Migration. Eine Handreichung für die Bildungspraxis. Bayerisches Staatsministerium für Arbeit und Soziales, Familie und Integration. Munich. https://www.hfph.de/forschung/wissenschaftliche-einrichtungen/globalefragen/nachrichten/handreichung-ab-sofort-zum-download-und-versand-erhaeltlich. Accessed 28 Feb 2020.

Klinkhammer, Gritt, and Anna Neumaier. 2020. *Religiöse Pluralitäten. Umbrüche in der Wahrnehmung religiöser Vielfalt in Deutschland*. Bielefeld: transcript.

Korteweg Anna C., and Gökce Yurdakul. 2016. *Kopftuchdebatten in Europa. Konflikte um Zugehörigkeit in nationalen Narrativen*. Bielefeld: transcript.

Lancy, David F. 2008. *The Anthropology of Childhood*. Cambridge: Cambridge University Press.

LAS (Leipziger Autoritarismus Studie). 2020. *Autoritäre Dynamiken. Alte Ressentiements – Neue Radikalität*, eds. Oliver Decker and Elmar Brähler. Gießen: Psychosozial-Verlag. https://www.boell.de/sites/default/files/2020-11/Decker-Braehler-2020-Autoritaere-Dynamiken-Leipziger-Autoritarismus-Studie.pdf. Accessed 28 Feb 2021.

LeVine, Robert A., and Rebecca S. New, eds. 2008. *Anthropology and Child Development. A Cross-Cultural Reader.* Malden: Blackwell Publishing.

Lingen-Ali, Ulrike, and Paul Mecheril, eds. 2020. Geschlechterdiskurse in der Migrationsgesellschaft. Zu „Rückständigkeit" und „Gefährlichkeit" der Anderen. Bielefeld: transcript.

Mitchell, J. Clyde. 1983. Case and Situation Analysis. *The Sociological Review* 31 (2): 187–211.

Müller, Kristin. 2013. Das Integrationspotenzial von Wohnungsgenossenschaften für türkischstämmige Migranten. In *Migrationsort Quartier. Zwischen Segregation, Integration und Interkultur.* eds. Olaf Schnur, Philipp Zakrzewski, and Matthias Drilling, 179–94. Wiesbaden: Springer VS.

Noelle-Neumann, Elisabeth. 1978. *Werden wir alle Proletarier? Wertewandel in unserer Gesellschaft.* Zürich: Edition Interfrom Zurich.

Ottersbach, Marcus, and Thomas Zitzmann, eds. 2009. *Jugendliche im Abseits. Zur Situation in französischen und deutschen marginalisierten Stadtquartieren.* Wiesbaden: VS Verlag.

Pettigrew, Thomas F., and Linda Tropp. 2006. A meta-analytic test of intergroup contact theory. *Journal of Personality and Social Psychology* 90 (5): 751–783.

Pollack, Detlef, and Olaf Müller. 2013. *Verstehen was verbindet. Religion und Zusammenhalt in Deutschland.* Gütersloh: Bertelsmann Stiftung.

Robert Bosch Stiftung, ed. 2019. Zusammenhalt in Vielfalt. Das Vielfaltsbarometer 2019 der Robert Bosch Stiftung. Stuttgart. https://www.bosch-stiftung.de/sites/default/files/publications/pdf/2019-03/Diversity%20Barometer%202019_Study%20Cohesion%20in%20Diversity.pdf. Accessed 28 Feb 2021.

Rössler, Martin. 2003. Die Extended-Case Methode. In *Methoden und Techniken der Feldforschung,* ed. Bettina Beer, 143–160. Berlin: Reimer Verlag.

Schnur, Olaf, Philipp Zakrzewski, and Matthias Drilling. 2013. *Migrationsort Quartier. Zwischen Segregation, Integration und Interkultur.* Wiesbaden: Springer VS.

Sinus Markt- und Sozialforschung. 2016. Sinus-Studie zu den Migranten-Lebenswelten in Deutschland 2016. http://www.sinus-institut.de/sinus-loesungen/sinus-migrantenmilieus/. Accessed 28 Feb 2021.

Stadtteilbüro Lenzsiedlung der Lawaetz-Stiftung, ed. 2007. *Aktive Stadtteilentwicklung in der Lenzsiedlung 2000 bis 2006. Die Lenzsiedlung – Die Queen Mary von Eimsbüttel.* Hamburg: commissioned by the Bezirksamt Eimsbüttel, Aktive Stadtteilentwicklung.

Statistikamt Nord. 2018. Social data of the statistical area 39010 (unpublished data).

Statistisches Bundesamt (Federal Statistical Office – Destatis) Migrationshintergrund. https://www.destatis.de/DE/Themen/Gesellschaft-Umwelt/Bevoelkerung/Migration-Integration/Glossar/migrationshintergrund.html. Accessed 14 July 2021.

Terkessidis, Mark. 2018. Harte Verhandlungen: über die Wertepluralität in einer Gesellschaft der Vielheit. In *Werte – Und was sie uns wert sind. Eine interdisziplinäre Anthologie,* eds. Randolf Rodenstock and Neşe Sevsay-Tegethoff, 109–125. Munich: Roman Herzog Institut e. V.

Uslucan, Haci-Halil. 2013. Lebenswelten und Werte von Migrantinnen. In *Dabeisein und Dazugehören. Integration in Deutschland*, eds. Heinz Ulrich Brinkmann and Haci-Halil Uslucan 227–248. Wiesbaden: Springer VS.
van Velsen, Jaap. 1967. The Extended-Case Method and Situational Analysis. In *The Craft of Social Anthropology*, ed. A.L. Epstein, 129–149. London: Tavistock.
Verein NL 40. 2011. Abschlussbericht „Oma/Opa-Projekt". Meilensteine – Umsetzung – Erfolge. February to June 2011. https://www.respekt.net/uploads/tx_alprojectfunding/RESPEKT_FINAL-2_GRANDMA_GRANDPA.pdf. Accessed 28 Feb 2021.
Werte-Index 2020. Published by Peter Wippermann and Jens Krüger. Frankfurt a. M.: Deutscher Fachverlag.
Wonneberger, Astrid, Diana Lölsdorf, Katja Weidtmann, and Sabina Stelzig. 2021. Der lange Schatten der Lenzsiedlung. Strategien zum Umgang mit Stigmatisierung in einer Großwohnsiedlung. *Standpunkt: sozial* 2021/3, 38–54.
Yildiz, Erol, and Marc Hill, eds. 2015. *Nach der Migration. Postmigrantische Perspektiven jenseits der Parallelgesellschaft*. Bielefeld: transcript.
Yildiz, Erol. 2015a. Postmigrantische Perspektiven. In *Nach der Migration. Postmigrantische Perspektiven jenseits der Parallelgesellschaft*. eds. Erol Yildiz and Marc Hill, 19–36. Bielefeld: transcript.
Yildiz, Miriam. 2015b. „Da sind wir Deutsche, hier sind wir Türken. Das ist schon manchmal schwer." Lebensstrategien Jugendlicher mit Migrationshintergrund in marginalisierten Stadtteilen: ein Perspektivwechsel. In *Nach der Migration. Postmigrantische Perspektiven jenseits der Parallelgesellschaft*. eds. Erol Yildiz and Marc Hill, 193–204. Bielefeld: transcript.
Zick, Andreas, and Nora Rebekka Krott, eds. 2021. Einstellungen zur Integration in der deutschen Bevölkerung von 2014 bis 2020. Studienbericht der vierten Erhebung im Projekt ZuGleich – Zugehörigkeit und Gleichwertigkeit. Bielefeld: IKG – Institut für interdisziplinäre Konflikt- und Gewaltforschung. https://www.stiftung-mercator.de/de/publikationen/einstellungen-zur-integration-in-der-deutschen-bevoelkerung-2021/. Accessed 16 Dec 2021.
Znidar, Ana. 2011. Großeltern unterrichten Migrantenkinder. Die Presse, June 22, 2011. https://www.respekt.net/uploads/tx_alprojectfunding/RESPEKT_FINAL-2_OMA_OPA.pdf. Accessed 1 Sept 2021.

PD Dr. Astrid Wonneberger *Department of Social Work, HAW Hamburg*
As a social and cultural anthropologist, Astrid Wonneberger has been a lecturer in the Applied Family Sciences program at the Hamburg University of Applied Sciences and a private lecturer at the Department of Social and Cultural Anthropology at the University of Hamburg since 2012. After many years of ethnographic field work in the Irish diaspora in the USA and in the Dublin Docklands, her academic interests focus on the topics of family, kinship and *community*, migration, diaspora, ethnicity, and urban anthropology. Since 2018, she has been part of the research team in the BMBF-project PoMiKu studying postmigrant family cultures in the Lenzsiedlung in the Hamburg district of Eimsbüttel.

Family in the Post-Migrant Society

Attitudes Towards Family Life in a High-Rise Housing Estate

Sabina Stelzig and Katja Weidtmann

> "There [at school] was a parent with his wife. Both came, I was alone. […] they spoke of the Lenzsiedlung and did not know that I am from the Lenzsiedlung [they said]: Oh, the families, who know nothing and whose children again so… I said, 'stop. If you know nothing, you can't say anything'."
> (Resident, 39 years old, born in Iran and raised in Germany, three children).[1]

1 Introduction

In politics and media, families as residents of large housing estates are often portrayed in a deficit-oriented way and in connection with a wide range of problems. Images of people in "incomplete" or "broken" families, of parents who show (too) little interest in their (too many) children and do not sufficiently fulfill their care and education duties dominate these presentations (cf. Keller 2015). Again and again, there is talk of children and adolescents with school problems and educational deficits, often in the context of educational distance or a weak socioeconomic status

---

[1] All interviews were conducted in German. The passages quoted in this article were translated by DEEPL and revised by the authors for accuracy. The same applies for all statements quoted from sources originally published in German.

S. Stelzig (✉) · K. Weidtmann
Department Soziale Arbeit, HAW Hamburg, Hamburg, Germany
e-mail: sabina.stelzig@haw-hamburg.de

K. Weidtmann
e-mail: katja.weidtmann@haw-hamburg.de

of their parents. The category "with a migratory background" quickly comes into focus in these debates. However, family life and family forms, potential problem situations, but also resources in high-rise housing estates are extremely diverse, particularly in families "with a migratory background" (Weber 2013, pp. 55–56).

For what reasons do people start a family or remain childless? Why do they enter or end partnerships? How do they develop certain expectations of gender roles in their partnership? And what are their ideas of how parents should interact with institutions such as daycare and school based on? Almost every part of family life is affected by such personal beliefs and societal representations. As a rule, numerous "family role models" are shared by many people within a society or within certain social groups. These "cultural" family role models, which are supposed to be characteristic for societies, regions, generations, or social milieus, are frequent subjects of research (Bundesinstitut für Bevölkerungsforschung 2017). However, it is by no means certain that differences in family-related values and norms can be attributed to a specific cultural origin ("with a migratory background"). Therefore, this article will investigate the thesis that apart from a specific cultural background other factors such as age, gender, living environment, neighborhood and community can also have an impact on behavioral norms and guiding values concerning family.

While the education and educational disadvantages of children from immigrant families have long been the subject of scientific publications, studies on immigrant families are still a relatively young field of research (cf. BMFSFJ 2016). Particularly family role models have only recently gained attention and been studied in families with a migratory background. In general, the heterogeneity of families with a migratory background cannot yet be fully displayed in empirical surveys, as the possibilities of differentiated queries in large surveys are rather limited. This limitation is addressed in the present article by reporting on the residents of a clearly defined area: the data basis for the following study is a survey of a total of 126 residents from the Lenzsiedlung, a high-rise housing estate in the west of Hamburg, which was conducted in 2020 as part of the BMBF project "Post-Migrant Family Cultures" (POMIKU).

The concept of a "post-migrant society" refers to a society that has accepted the fact that it has been transformed by immigration and emigration into a culturally diverse society, regardless of whether this process is positively or negatively evaluated by its members and institutions. In terms of numbers, Germany is one of the most important countries of destination for international migrants worldwide. Almost 13.8 million people residing in Germany have immigrated. In 40 percent of all family households with minor children, at least one family member has a migratory background (BMFSFJ 2021).

The postulate of a post-migrant society describes a society "after politics has realized that Germany has become a country of immigration or—even more—an immigrant society" (Broden and Mecheril 2007), which is characterized by immigration and emigration, as Foroutan et al. write in their study on attitudes of the Muslim community in Hamburg (Foroutan et al. 2014, p. 10). The authors also take the position that in political and public perception, it has been accepted that migration is not a temporary phenomenon, but will eventually "lead to a structural, social, cultural, and emotional transformation of the economy, politics and the society" (ibid.).

The aim of this article is to describe and analyze the family role models of the residents in a high-rise housing estate and to question the popular assumption that the cultural origin ("migration background") determines family role models. Methodologically, this research has applied items on family role models that have been proven useful in previous studies. Three main categories help to structure the questionnaire: firstly, it asks questions about "attitudes to belonging to and boundaries of family", secondly about "functions of family", and thirdly about "gender role models". The division into these three subjects serves as a theoretical framework and helps to structure the items. The contents may overlap.

The article starts by pointing out the relevance of research on family role models, particularly for the study of families in a high-rise housing estate. It also describes how the rather dazzling term "family role models" was made fruitful for the research. After that, the mixed-method approach consisting of a standardized survey, guideline interviews, expert interviews, and participant observation is described. The presentation of the collected data, their analysis and the description of the results are based on the three main categories presented above. Finally, it should become clear how important it is to detach a detailed exploration of family role models in large housing estates from established dichotomous categories of people "with and without a migratory background".[2]

2 On the Term "Role Models"

The concept of role models has its origin in psychology and sociology. Both disciplines have differentiated its use further and developed different understandings of the term (Pardo-Puhlmann et al. 2016, p. 2ff.). At this point, however, these

---

[2] Thanks to Nora Zimmer for her diverse support for this contribution.

differences will not be discussed any further, as only the common features of both approaches will be used as guiding principles for this contribution. For example, from both a psychological and sociological perspective, it is important to know how societal role models are generally acquired by individuals and to what extent culture determines individual role models (Giesel 2007, p. 60).

Without further differentiating the use of the term, we consider role models as "constructs that influence family life, gender relations, and the development of families by prescribing patterns of action that are considered desirable, worthwhile, and achievable" (cf. Schneider and Diabaté 2020, p. 1). From the variety of meanings of the term, we will follow the specification of Diabaté and Lück (2014, p. 56). They define role models as "a bundle of collectively shared images of the 'normal', that is, of something desirable, socially accepted and/or presumably widespread, i.e. self-evident" (ibid.). That means, role models serve as central orientations in everyday life. For Schneider and Diabaté (2020, p. 4) role models are "accordingly based on the connection of different facets of values, norms, and frames.[3] Role models are complex visualizations that serve both people and organizations for orientation. As a central feature, family role models are intersubjectively shared and characteristically constituted for different collectives."

According to this view, role models create a consensus within a society or within a certain social milieu. They can be characterized by a great homogeneity and support homogeneity in societies or social milieus. Role models often vary between different collectives, e.g. between different cultures and/or religious groups, between different age groups, generations, gender groups, or social milieus (Schneider et al. 2015). However, role models providing orientation for behavior can also be observed at an individual level: They can serve as an important framework of orientation in everyday life by prescribing action scripts. Different role models, sometimes even contradictory role models, often exist side by side. The example of "modern parenthood" illustrates this: according to this role model, mothers and fathers should always care for their children in every respect and at the same time be successful in professional full-time jobs. Role models are very important for the design of family life, as Schneider and Diabaté (2020, p. 3) explain: According to them, role models "in their interaction shape the family and gender culture, partner relationships and living together, the social construction of childhood and parenthood and thus the relationship between different generations". Family role models often gain an independent reality through a daily

---

[3] Following Esser's (1990) theory of frame selection, "frames" refer to culturally shaped categories of situations, for which a corresponding script was created.

social reproduction and their institutionalization (Lück and Diabaté 2014; Lück et al. 2017). This particularly affects the socially shaped gender relations within the family. The concept of role models is extended by Pfau-Effinger (2004) as "typical societal ideal representations, norms, and values regarding the family and the societal integration of women and men" (Pfau-Effinger 2004, p. 82).

Individual and social role models mutually influence each other. Individual family role models originate primarily in one's family of origin and the immediate social environment, where attitudes and behavior are learned as "natural". The groups representing them try to enforce the acceptance and validity of their role models, sometimes against the resistance of others. This becomes obvious, for example, in many emotionally charged discussions about parental responsibility or gender roles. The debate about the "correct" start of institutional care for infants or toddlers is referred to here as an example (Gerlach 2017; cf. also Schneider et al. 2015, p. 11).

In summary, family role models arise from observation and from the idea of what most people in society believe, think, and do. Many people consider their models as appropriate and therefore good and right. Such notions of normality consciously and unconsciously shape people's actions.

3 Study Design and Operationalization

The Lenzsiedlung in Hamburg-Eimsbüttel was erected between 1974 and 1984 as a social housing project. With around 2800 people (in 2020) in an area of 7.6 hectares, it is one of the most densely populated districts in Hamburg. Its residents are characterized, among other things, by an above-average proportion of families: the rate of households with minor children is 28 percent, compared to 18 percent in Hamburg as a whole. A third of these family households are single-parent households, about three times as many as in the entire Hamburg city area. Over 70 percent of the residents having a migratory background,[4] twice as many compared to the city of Hamburg. Among the minors, almost 84 percent have a migratory background in comparison to about 50 percent in Hamburg as a whole (in 2019). The cultural diversity is shaped by people from over 60 countries of origin (Statistikamt Nord 2021).

---

[4] A "migratory background" is attributed to a person who was born without German citizenship or who has at least one parent to whom this characteristic applies (Statistisches Bundesamt 2018). The term is used critically in this contribution (see below).

The results on family role models presented here are based on a standardized online survey with 107 residents of the Lenzsiedlung, which was conducted between October 2020 and March 2021. Due to the Covid-19 pandemic, the study, which had originally been planned as a door-to-door survey, was conducted as an online/paper-and-pencil survey. For this purpose, a letter containing a link to the online survey and a paper questionnaire with return postage was sent to all adult residents of the housing estate. The survey consists of ten items on attitudes towards family life and nine socio-demographic questions. The questions and scales were mostly taken from the Family Models Study of the Bundesinstitut für Bevölkerungsforschung (BiB) 2013 (BiB 2013; cf. Lück and Diabaté 2015). Some questions were slightly adapted. Further selected scales were taken from the Survey Database of the German Youth Institute (DJI 2014), the Educare Project (de Moll et al. 2016) and the Data Report 2018 (Statistisches Bundesamt and Wissenschaftszentrum Berlin für Sozialforschung 2018), based on questions from the General Population Survey of the Social Sciences (ALLBUS) in 2012 and 2016. This selection was intended to cover a broad spectrum of central family-relevant topics with only a few questions. The questions are assigned to the three analysis categories mentioned above, which can partially overlap: "Belonging to and boundaries of family" includes questions such as: What is a family? Who belongs to it? What criteria define a family? A second focus is the category "family functions": What functions are families expected to fulfil? What should be done in the family and with family members? What should family members do for each other? One focus of this category deals with growing up and raising children. And thirdly, the topic of "intra-family roles" will be looked at, which includes questions as to which family member ideally performs which function? What is an "appropriate" task for him or her, and what is not?

The return of the standardized survey was just over five percent (107 respondents out of 2008 contacted residents), which might be explained by the unavoidable switch from a door-to-door survey to a written survey. The latter would probably have resulted in a higher return, as filling in a multi-page written questionnaire might have been a hurdle for many people (see below). The presentation of the results starts with the outcomes for all respondents concerning the categories outlined above, before possible differences between the answers of men and women, different age groups, people with a non-German or German first language, and people with Turkish or German first language are discussed.

What characteristics do the respondents have? Two thirds of the participants are female. The age structure corresponds to that of the adults in the housing estate. The 40- to 50-year-olds, however, are slightly overrepresented in the survey[5] (Statistikamt Nord 2021). Around two thirds have lived in the Lenzsiedlung for more than ten years. A quarter of the respondents live as singles; about three quarters live in a partnership. Five percent live with four adults, more than 30 percent with minor children in the household. Ten respondents were single parents.

Two thirds of the respondents speak German as their first language, almost every fourth person Turkish. Other frequently mentioned first languages are Farsi and Arabic. English is often spoken in addition to the first language. Spanish and French are also frequently mentioned as second languages. People of Turkish descent represent one of the largest groups with a migratory background in Germany and this is also true for the Lenzsiedlung. For this reason, potential differences between residents with Turkish and German first language were also examined.

Almost half of those who filled out the questionnaire (multiple answers possible) mainly finance themselves through their wages. 28 percent of the respondents are retired, and 14 percent receive social welfare benefits. About eight percent have a mini-job and another seven percent receive unemployment benefits. Five percent are self-employed or receive support from their family.

For a further differentiation of the findings at the individual level, 28 guideline interviews were used. They were conducted with female residents from 27 to 85 years of age between 2019 and 2020 and dealt with various general aspects of "family life". These data were supplemented with information from interviews on "living in the Lenzsiedlung", which were conducted with five professional psycho-social counselors, who were working in adjacent neighborhoods of the Lenzsiedlung. The recorded interviews are between 45 and 120 min long.

The fact that just over 80 percent of the minor population has a "migratory background" points at a high proportion of second and third generation migrants in the estate. However, the category "with a migratory background" is often criticized. As Will (2020) writes, this classification marks a boundary between Germans with and without a migratory background. "Many people born and raised in Germany as German citizens are made 'foreigners' by their migratory background", he continues. The majority of the 5.2 million people in this category have only one parent who was naturalized, who immigrated as a resettler ("Aussiedler") or who still has a foreign citizenship (Statistisches Bundesamt 2019).

---

[5] The respondents belonged to the following age groups: 16–30 years ($n=14$), 31–40 years ($n=17$), 41–50 years ($n=24$), 51–60 years ($n=18$), 61–70 years ($n=12$), 71 years and older ($n=17$).

Although their individual life experiences are likely to differ greatly, all these people are classified under the same category, which also includes people who have immigrated from abroad, refugees, and asylum seekers.

The main characteristics for attributing a "migratory background" to a respondent in the micro-census are the place of birth (in Germany or abroad) and whether the German citizenship was acquired by birth or naturalization (Statistisches Bundesamt 2019). The present study tries to achieve a more adequate differentiation by asking for the characteristic "first language" instead of "origin/ descent". The underlying assumption is that the first language corresponds to the cultural background of the family.

From a methodological point of view, it must be critically noted that residents with a non-German first language are somewhat underrepresented in this study compared to the entire population of the housing estate (cf. Statistikamt Nord 2021). This includes the Turkish-speaking population. A later translation of the questionnaire into Turkish did not increase the response rate. Especially for people who have limited to no proficiency in reading longer texts and documents in German, the written format of the survey posed a barrier to participation. This was also confirmed by several counselors working in various social services centers in the urban quarter.

The following sections present the results of the surveys along the three investigated thematic foci, namely "attitudes towards belonging to and boundaries of family", "functions of family" and "relationship of the role of women and men in the family". The data are then analyzed in terms of similarities and differences concerning gender, age, and cultural origin/descent (resp. first language). Further characteristics that can influence the residents' role models about family will be derived from the in-depth interviews at the end of this article.

4 Attitudes Towards Belonging to and Boundaries of Family

As the first step, the study examined what social life forms the respondents consider as family (focus "belonging to and boundaries of family"). Based on the study "Familienleitbilder" of the BiB (Schneider et al. 2015), the first question asked—using predefined categories—what the group of people looks like that forms a family. For this purpose, the respondents were asked to classify seven different forms of social groups as "yes, this is a family" or "no, this is not a family". Scaling the answers was not possible (Fig. 1).

While family is for most respondents—not exclusively—a married couple consisting of a man and a woman, who live together with their own children

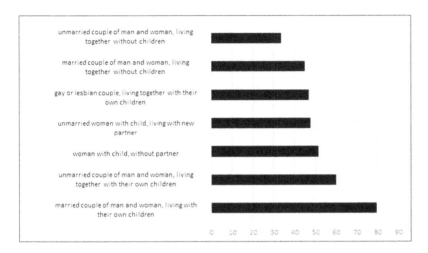

Fig. 1 Ideas of family: "yes, this is a family" (n = 107, multiple answers possible, data in %); source of scale: BiB (2013). *Source*: figure created by the authors

(about 80 percent), for significantly more than half of the respondents the term family is not tied to a marriage certificate, but an unmarried couple with children can also be a family. It becomes clear that the orientation towards the nuclear family of recent decades still exists, but the residents are quite open to diverse family forms. This result can be underlined by the finding that the long prevailing norm which prescribes marriage before having children is widely rejected. Only 20 percent agreed to this statement, as will be shown in more detail later. This finding is consistent with the observation that the concept of family in Germany in the first post-war decades has long been oriented towards marriage as the main criterion. To date, however, almost any social group with responsibilities between parents and children is considered a family (Schneider 2008).

The characteristic of generativity is considered more important for the designation as a "family" than the presence of a parental couple. This is also underlined by the fact that half of the respondents agree on the statement that a woman with a child without a partner also represents a family.

Comparing the responses of women and men to the question of what a family is hardly shows any differences. Only an "unmarried, cohabiting couple consisting of a man and a woman without children" is regarded as a family by more men than women (Table 1). In a representative survey by the FLB (2012, 2016), however, this result is exactly the opposite: more women than men consider this constellation as a family. It is assumed that there is a tendency to see one's own social life form more as "a family" than other forms (Schneider et al. 2015, p. 73), although the causality is not clear: "Either the experience of living in a certain social life form leads to regarding this life form as a family. Or the existing ideal of a family leads to choosing a certain social life form or accepting it (especially since social life forms are often not freely chosen). There are probably mutual influences." Regardless of gender, this finding might also apply to the following results.

Interestingly, in the Lenzsiedlung not only older residents, but also younger respondents have a rather conservative image of family, which is closely aligned with the traditional nuclear family. Thus, when the six age groups are compared, the youngest and the two oldest groups tend to see the following social life forms less as families than the two middle age groups: "woman with child without partner", "woman with child, unmarried, cohabiting with new partner" and "unmarried couple consisting of a man and a woman, cohabiting, without children" (Table 1).

An explanatory hypothesis can be seen in the fact that, on the one hand, older respondents are probably more strongly influenced by the image of the "classic" nuclear family, which was dominant until a decade ago, in which a married heterosexual couple living together raised children. On the other hand, aspects of stability and security in relationships are again playing an increasingly important role for the younger generation in founding a family today. In their perception, both seem to be more likely to be found through an orientation towards traditional family role models (Albert et al. 2019; Koppetsch 2014).

The following passage from a guideline interview illustrates the traditional notions of normative ideas of "proper" families with which older residents were socialized:

> "Originally I come from C. [place in Germany]. Then I had my daughter out of wedlock, and my brother's wife said they couldn't go out on the street in C. anymore because I have an illegitimate child and he is the Mr. engineer—and since then my relationship with them has become very distant." (Resident, 75 years old, born and raised in Germany)

Another possible explanation for why the middle age group has less conservative ideas about belonging to a family than the younger group could be that they are more likely to have experienced critical family events such as separation or divorce, phases of single parenthood or constellations of step-parenthood, either

Table 1 Degree of agreement with the statement, "yes, this is a family"; group comparisons by gender and age (selection)

Unmarried, cohabiting couple consisting of a man and a woman without children

	Not a family		Family		Chi^2-test			
	%	n	%	n	Value	df	p	phi
Women	71.4	50	28.6	20	3.73	1	0.045	0.19
Men	51.6	16	48.4	15				

Notes: n = 70 women; n = 31 men; Chi^2-test according to Pearson

Woman with child without a partner

Age group	No family		Family		Chi^2-test			
	%	n	%	n	Value	df	p	Cramer-V
16–30 years	57.1	8	42.9	6	22.42	5	0.000	0.47
31–40 years	23.5	4	76.5	13				
41–50 years	25.0	6	75.0	18				
51–60 years	44.4	8	55.6	10				
61–70 years	66.7	8	33.3	4				
71 years and older	88.2	15	11.8	2				

Unmarried woman with a child, living with a new partner

Age group	No family		Family		Chi^2-test			
	%	n	%	n	Value	df	p	Cramer-V
16–30 years	64.3	9	35.7	5	12.88	5	0.025	0.36
31–40 years	29.4	5	70.6	12				
41–50 years	33.3	8	66.7	16				
51–60 years	55.6	10	44.4	8				
61–70 years	66.7	8	33.3	4				
71 years and older	76.5	13	23.5	4				

(continued)

Table 1 (continued)

Unmarried couple consisting of a man and a woman, living together, without children

Age group	No family		Family		Chi^2-test			
	%	n	%	n	Value	df	p	Cramer-V
16–30 years	85.7	12	14.3	2	13.95	5	0.016	0.37
31–40 years	41.2	7	58.8	10				
41–50 years	50.0	12	50.0	12				
51–60 years	66.7	12	33.3	6				
61–70 years	75.0	9	25.0	3				
71 years and older	88.2	15	11.8	2				

$n=14$ 16–30 years; $n=17$ 31–40 years; $n=24$ 41–50 years; $n=18$ 51–60 years; $n=12$ 61–70 years; $n=17$ 71 years and older; Chi^2-Test according to Pearson

themselves or in their social environment. These experiences might have helped to diversify their ideas of a "normal" family over time.

Statements from the explorative guideline interviews also show that there are extreme differences within the resident population in terms of evaluating the importance of biological kinship as a criterion for family membership. Some see this criterion as indispensable for a definition of family, while others completely reject it. Especially in connection with migration, the discussion about the criterion of biological kinship ("blood relationship") for the concept of family becomes important, as the following statement illustrates:

> "That means, the family is always the most important thing. I also have many friends and so on, but the family is, because it is blood. […] I came here because of my mother. Because I am the only child and there was no one else and […] I thought, my mother, she really needs me, because there is no one for her here. […] But you can replace a husband or friend or wife, but you can't replace a mother. That's why I decided to come here. […] (Resident, 71 years old, born in Germany, returned from the USA after about 40 years)

The social relationships between people of two generations can also be decisive for the designation of a family, regardless of biological kinship, sometimes even without a legal framework:

> "I have him (laughs) not legally adopted, but adopted, like that. He didn't have a mother, she died, the father was so-so, so I took him in and raised him as my child.

And I went with him to the doctor and to school, everything you do for your own child, I did for him, and he is now 27." (Resident, mid-30s, born and raised in Armenia)

What is striking here is that the cultural origin of the two interviewees with their opposing positions regarding the significance of biological kinship for family membership often contradicts observed stereotypes of western-liberal or secular and thus supposedly more open attitudes towards traditional-religious family relationships, which could be attributed to the cultural background of the interviewee from the second example.

Statements from the residents suggest that households with migration and refugee experiences occasionally provide shelter for relatives or acquaintances in case of homelessness due to persecution and displacement in their country of origin, for instance. These experiences might also have shaped the idea of "who does and does not belong to the family". That means, role models influence actions, but action-based experiences, such as the need to support someone in case of (forced) migration, can also influence one's family role models and what they are supposed to perform:

"So [we live in] one and a half rooms and then his nephew comes... without papers, without anything. [...] to Italy over the sea from Tunisia, illegally, and then he is here in Hamburg. [...] but one month, one week, two weeks [...] four months with me. It's too much. [...] I, okay, you are the uncle, of course you take him in, because he is his nephew. I understand that. [...] It was in August [the youngest daughter] was born. And cleaning, cooking. He smokes cigarettes. He has no money, nothing at all. He is—nothing. And here in Germany, he just sits there. If he is sick... I don't know what he should do." (Resident, late 20s, born and raised in Tunisia, five children)

The survey also shows that people with a non-German first language hold a slightly more conservative family role model than people with German as their first language: Thus, respondents without German as their first language regard an unmarried, cohabiting couple without children less often as a family (Table 2). However, there were no significant differences between people with Turkish and German as their first language. Unlike the study of Diabaté et al. (2016), marriage here does not seem to play a crucial role for native Turkish speakers.

Based on the repeatedly observed finding that during phases of single parenting, families, especially single mothers, have fewer financial resources available than two-parent families (Lenze 2021; Lenze and Funcke 2016; Peuckert 2012), it is very likely that such families move into housing estates where rents are affordable and

Table 2 Comparison between people with a non-German and German first language "yes, this is a family: unmarried, cohabiting couple without children". Notes: n = 36 non-German first language; n = 69 first language German; Chi^2 test according to Pearson

First language	"no family"		"family"		Chi^2 -test			
	%	n	%	n	value	df	p	phi
Non-German	77.8	28	22.2	8	3.28	1	0.054	−0.180
German	60.0	39	40.0	26				

rent control is high. Therefore, it is not surprising that twice as many single parents as in the rest of the Lokstedt district lived in the Lenzsiedlung in 2019 (Statistikamt Nord 2021). This may lead to increased contacts with single-parent families and thus to a more "open family role model" which includes single parents.

Whether contacts between different family forms lead to a greater tolerance in terms of personal role models or, on the contrary, reinforce existing normative beliefs by referring to perceived boundaries, needs to be further examined. On the one hand, the density of contacts between many residents of the Lenzsiedlung, especially of households with minor children, is repeatedly described as "quite high" by residents, community workers, and the youth welfare office. Therefore, it can be assumed that neighborhood exchange and support are likely and part of everyday life. The surrounding green spaces, smaller play areas and the large playgrounds in the center of the housing estate, which are available for sports and leisure activities, are likely to promote further contacts between families. On the other hand, however, it should also be noted that residents also report of families whose networks do not stretch beyond their own ethnic community or who live rather isolated. Their role models are not very likely to be influenced by neighborhood contacts. These considerations will be taken up again later.

5 Attitudes Towards the Functions of Family

Figure 2 indicates that all respondents, regardless of their cultural background, show a high level of agreement regarding the functions resp. importance of children. Most respondents express great joy in seeing them grow up and regard it as important that fathers take on family tasks. The statements that women should not have children if they aspire to a professional career and that children represent a financial burden which restricts the standard of living are most strongly rejected.

Family in the Post-Migrant Society   117

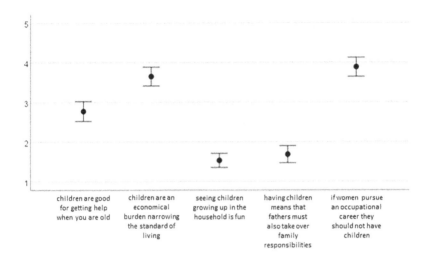

Fig. 2 Importance of children: "What do children mean to you personally?" (5-point response scale from 1 ("completely agree") to 5 ("do not agree at all"); n = 107 (all respondents); circle: arithmetic mean, bar: 95% confidence interval of the arithmetic mean; item list based on DJI-Survey (2014). *Source*: figure created by the authors

While there are no significant differences regarding gender and age, a higher rate of agreement exists among Turkish-speaking respondents when asked about the importance of children. More people with Turkish than with German as their first language agree with the statement "children are good for getting help when you are old" (Table 3). Apart from the culturalist thesis which assumes a generally stronger family orientation among families of Turkish descent, there are also alternative explanations: Having grown up with the experiences of their own (1st generation) parents that the state only provides limited services in old age, children are regarded as a potential source of support in this respect.

Turkish-speaking respondents agree to a larger extent with the statement that "parents should provide their children with a variety of leisure activities" than German-speaking residents. German speakers, however, agree more with the statement "children should rather play with other children than with their parents". These findings are consistent with studies that notice a stronger family orientation in relation to other family topics among people of Turkish descent compared to those of German descent (Schenk and Habermann 2020; BMFSFJ 2016; Janßen and Polat 2006). Even higher levels of agreement with the statement "having

Table 3 Comparison between Turkish and German first language speakers regarding their attitudes towards "importance of children" and "demands on parental performance today". *Notes: n = 16 first language Turkish; n = 69 first language German; 5-point response scale from 1 ("completely agree") to 5 ("do not agree at all"); t-test for independent samples; case exclusion listwise; significance test two-sided at 5% level*

	First language Turkish			First language German			t-test			
	n	m	sd	n	m	sd	t	df	p	d
"Having children in the household and seeing them grow up is fun"	14	1.0	0.000	56	1.5	0.831	4.66	55	0.000	0.33
"Children are good for getting help when you are old"	14	1.6	1.151	56	3.2	1.04	4.78	68	0.000	0.58
"Parents should provide their children with a variety of leisure activities"	14	1.3	0.469	57	2.1	0.766	3.98	69	0.000	0.51
"Children should rather play with other children than with their parents"	14	3.4	1.008	57	2.5	0.848	-3.30	69	0.002	0.44

children in the household and seeing them grow up is fun" among Turkish speaking respondents seem to further underline this thesis (Table 3). Differentiating between gender and age groups does not make any difference regarding these findings.

Further questions about the functions of the family focused on ideas about what parents should do to support their children between zero and ten years of age. Figure 3 shows that all respondents consider obtaining information about the "right upbringing" and the conscious, early arrangement of learning opportunities for children more important than blaming parents for the academic failure of children due to a lack of care or insufficient interest in their children's learning progress.

Women reject the idea that parents are responsible for their children's academic failure due to a lack of care more strongly than men. The comparison between people with a non-German and German first language reveals a significant difference in the item "lack of parental interest in the child's learning progress is decisive for academic failure"; the former reject this statement more strongly than the latter (Table 4). As far as the item "poor school performance is caused by a lack of parental interest in the academic success of their children" is

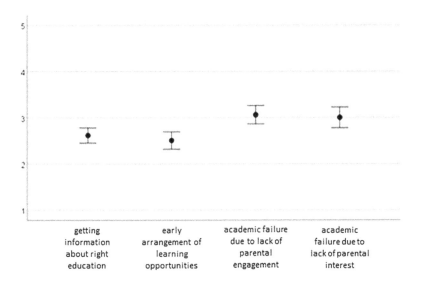

Fig. 3 Attitudes towards parents as learning arrangers: "There are different opinions about what parents should do to support their children from 0 to 10 years. What is your opinion on this topic?" (5-point response scale from 1 ("completely agree") to 5 ("do not agree at all"); n = 107 all respondents; circle: arithmetic mean, bar: 95% confidence interval of the arithmetic mean; item list based on de Moll et al. (2016). Source: figure created by the authors

Table 4 Comparison by gender and first language regarding "what parents should do to support their children from 0 to 10 years of age"; 5-level response scale from 1 ("completely agree") to 5 ("do not agree at all"); t-test for independent samples; listwise exclusion of cases; significance test two-sided at 5% level

Academic failure due to lack of parental engagment									
women			men			t-test			
n	M	SD	n	M	SD	t	df	p	d
66	3.2	0.957	30	2.8	0.971	2.18	94	0.032	0.23

$n=70$ women; $n=31$ men

Non-German first language			first language German			t-test			
n	M	SD	n	M	SD	t	df	p	d
32	2.7	0.865	64	3.3	0.974	3.23	94	0.002	0.33

$n=36$ non-German first language; $n=69$ first language German

concerned, differences between various age groups can be noticed, but no clear age-dependent trend can be identified.

Turkish-speaking respondents consider parents more responsible for supporting their children in terms of school performance German first language speakers. The former agreed more strongly with the statement that parents "should arrange learning opportunities for their children from an early age" and "should have time in the afternoon to help their children with learning". Therefore, it is not surprising that Turkish-speaking respondents hold parents more responsible for their children's school performance than German speaking respondents. They also agreed more often with the statement "children fail in school because their parents do not take care enough of school matters" (Table 5).

At first glance, these results are consistent with findings from studies that show a stronger general family orientation among people of Turkish descent (Schenk and Habermann 2020; BMFSFJ 2016; Janßen and Polat 2006). This also applies for education. However, it should be considered that particularly first-generation Turkish migrants often have a relatively low level of education due to their recruitment as laborers. Attributing the responsibility for children's academic success to their parents alone could thus also be interpreted as a cultural transmission, in the sense that the first generation has consciously or unconsciously passed on the task of compensating for any existing (educational) disadvantages in today's school children to the second generation, or that the second generation has taken on this task due to their own family's educational biography.

Table 5 Comparison between people with Turkish and German as their first language regarding "what parents should do to support their children from 0 to 10 years of age"; items based on FLB 2012, 2016 (Lück and Diabaté 2015); n = 16 first language Turkish; n = 69 first language German; 5-point response scale from 1 ("completely agree") to 5 ("do not agree at all"); t-test for independent samples; case exclusion listwise; significance test two-sided at 5% level

	First language Turkish			First language German			t-test			
	n	M	SD	n	M	SD	t	df	p	d
Arrange learning opportunities for their children from an early age	14	2.1	0.829	59	2.6	0.889	2.13	71	0.037	0.30
Having time in the afternoon to help children with their learning	14	1.5	0.760	57	2.4	0.896	3.27	69	0.002	0.46
Academic failure due to lack of parental engagement	14	2.6	1.082	59	3.3	0.976	2.35	71	0.022	0.33

Despite all efforts in recent years, educational opportunities in Germany are still unevenly distributed, especially regarding differences depending on the socio-economic status of the parents (Autorengruppe Bildungsberichterstattung 2020). In 2018, the PISA survey once again showed that the correlation between a child's reading competence and structural characteristics such as origin/descent and educational background of its parents is much stronger in Germany than in the OECD average (see AID: A 2019).

In addition to the socio-economic disparities, there are also large differences between children with and without a migratory background. It should also not be forgotten that there are very large differences between the individual countries of origin in terms of the level of education. The AID: A-Survey (2019, p. 39) concludes that "the well-known finding that people with a migratory background have lower educational opportunities not only refers to the absolute educational level of the target persons [...], but also to their educational mobility in relation to their parents. People with a migratory background, and especially those with a bilateral migratory background, show slightly less educational advancements and significantly more educational declines." Given this fact, it is not surprising that in the present study a "good school performance" is considered more important by many families with a migratory background than by Germans.

> "But I fight, and I fight. If my children are good in school, then I say, yes (sighs of relief). Now I have succeeded. [...] My wish is that my children graduate from high school. Good. When they have grown up, that each has a good job and that they are on a right way." (Resident, late 20s, born and raised in Tunisia, five children)

This result also applies to many families of Turkish descent, and it is confirmed by results from the survey on the importance of certain educational goals (Table 9).

The set of questions dealing with familial support of children from a deficit-oriented perspective reveal a generally positive attitude towards the corresponding familial options (Fig. 4). It becomes clear that particularly value transmission takes place within families rather than institutions.

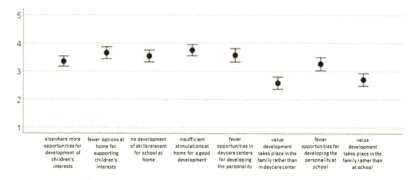

Fig. 4 Familial support: "Family life can be very diverse. We are interested in what children do, learn, and experience in families. How much do you agree with the following statements?" (5-point response scale from 1 ("completely agree") to 5 ("do not agree at all"); n = 107 all respondents; circle: arithmetic mean, bar: 95% confidence interval of the arithmetic mean; item list based on de Moll et al. (2016). *Source*: figure created by the authors

Table 6 What children do, learn, and experience in the family: Comparison between people with and without German first language; n = 36 non-German first language; n = 69 first language German; 5-point response scale from 1 ("completely agree") to 5 ("do not agree at all"); t-test for independent samples; case exclusion listwise; significance test two-sided at 5% level

	Non-German first language			First language German			t-test			
	n	M	SD	n	M	SD	t	df	p	d
"insufficient opportunities at home to support children in their interests"	25	3.2	0.779	59	3.8	1.072	2.50	61	0.015	0.25

There are no systematic differences in terms of gender and age. German first language speakers are less likely to think that they have insufficient opportunities at home to promote their children's interests than non-German first language speakers (Table 6). More people with Turkish as their first language agree with the statement that daycare provides children with fewer opportunities for personal development than the family, compared to native German speakers (Table 7).

The education of children is still seen as one of the most important functions of the family (Wonneberger and Stelzig-Willutzki 2018). Therefore, the present study also asked which educational goals are important for a ten-year-old child today. As Fig. 5 shows for all respondents, all goals mentioned in the questionnaire are considered quite significant. The average ratings are all situated in the lower half of the scale. The most important items are "self-confidence", "understanding for others", "good manners", and "sense of responsibility", while "diligence", "good school performance", "modesty", and "obedience" are named less frequently.

A comparative look at the answers depending on gender shows that women consider the following goals as more important than men: "understanding for others", "ability to criticize" and "sense of responsibility". There is a significant age-related difference only in the educational goal "obedience", although there is no clear trend visible. However, it is interesting that this goal is considered most important by the youngest group (between 16 and 30 years of age) and least important by the oldest group (over 70 years of age).

Table 7 What children do, learn, and experience in the family: Comparison between respondents with Turkish and German first language; n = 16 first language Turkish; n = 69 first language German; 5-point response scale from 1 ("completely agree") to 5 ("do not agree "not at all"); t-test for independent samples; case exclusion listwise; significance test two-sided at 5% level

	First language Turkish			First language German			t-test			
	n	M	SD	n	M	SD	t	df	p	d
"daycare provides fewer opportunities for personality development than the family"	12	2.8	0.937	54	3.6	1.160	2.01	64	0.048	0.31

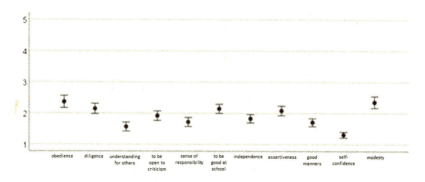

Fig. 5 Relevance of educational goals: "How important do you consider the following educational goals for a 10-year-old child today?" (5-point response scale from 1 ("completely agree") to 5 ("do not agree at all"); n = 107 all respondents; circle: arithmetic mean, bar: 95% confidence interval of the arithmetic mean; item list based on Kohn (1959, 1969; Kohn and Schoenbach 1986, cf. also Bertram 1991, p. 437). *Source*: figure created by the authors

People with non-German and German first language rate the educational goals "diligence" and "obedience" differently: non-German speakers consider these goals more relevant than native German speakers (Table 8).

Table 8 Relevance of educational goals: Comparison between people with non-German vs. German first language in terms of "relevance of educational goals for 10-year-old children today"; n=36 non-German first language; n=69 first language German; 5-level response scale from 1 ("completely agree") to 5 ("do not agree at all"); t-test for independent samples; case exclusion listwise; significance test two-sided at 5% level

	Non-German first language			First language German			t-test			
	n	M	SD	n	M	SD	t	df	p	d
Obedience	31	2.5	0.948	60	2.0	0.948	2.31	89	0.023	0.25
Diligence	31	2.4	0.755	60	1.7	0.729	3.68	89	0.000	0.37

Apart from "school performance", the items "diligence" and "obedience" seem to be particularly contested in terms of educational goals in families. Turkish-speaking respondents attribute a higher priority to these items than German native speakers (Table 9).

For parenting behavior, these ideas (with a stronger focus on diligence and obedience) might imply a higher probability for a more authoritarian parenting style. However, physical violence and punishment in education is more strongly rejected by Turkish than by German native speakers (Table 10).

Overall, the answers show that all respondents clearly reject violence and physical punishment as a means in raising children (Fig. 6).

While no age-related differences can be observed here, a look at "gender" shows that women are less tolerant towards occasional slaps. Furthermore, people with a non-German first language are more likely to demand a general prohibition

Table 9 Relevance of educational goals: Comparison between people with Turkish and German as their first language regarding the "relevance of educational goals for 10-year-old children today"; n=16 first language Turkish; n=69 first language German; 5-level response scale from 1 ("completely agree") to 5 ("do not agree at all"); t-test for independent samples; case exclusion listwise; significance test two-sided at 5% level

	First language Turkish			First language German			t-test			
	n	M	SD	n	M	SD	t	df	p	d
Good school performance	14	1.9	0.770	55	2.3	0.695	2.21	67	0.030	0.31
Obedience	14	1.8	0.893	55	2.5	0.900	2.69	67	0.009	0.37
Diligence	14	1.5	0.650	55	2.4	0.735	4.18	67	0.000	0.50

Table 10 Physical violence and punishment in raising children: Comparison between people with Turkish and German as their first language on "what is your opinion on physical punishment in raising children?"; n = 16 first language Turkish; n = 69 first language German; 5-point response scale from 1 ("strongly agree") to 5 ("strongly disagree"); t-test for independent samples; case exclusion listwise; significance test two-sided at 5% level

	First language Turkish			First language German			t-test			
	n	M	SD	n	M	SD	t	df	p	d
Prohibition of physical violence	14	1.0	0.000	59	1.6	1.052	4.33	58	0.000	0.63
Occasional slaps are okay	14	4.9	0.535	59	4.3	1.027	2.64	39	0.012	0.63
Physical violence is okay in certain situations	14	5.0	0.000	59	4.3	1.004	5.32	58	0.000	0.77

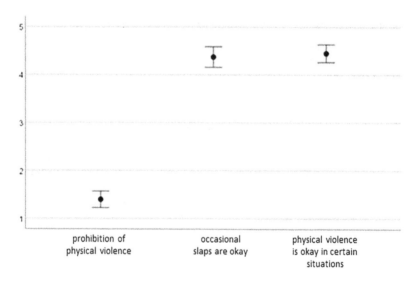

Fig. 6 Physical violence and punishment in raising children: "What is your opinion on physical punishment as a means of raising children?" (5-point response scale from 1 ("strongly agree") to 5 ("strongly disagree"); n = 107 all respondents; circle: arithmetic mean, bar: 95% confidence interval of the arithmetic mean; own scale. *Source*: figure created by the authors

Table 11 Physical violence in raising children: Comparison between persons with non-German and German first language speakers on "what is your opinion on using occasional slaps in raising children?"; n = 36 non-German first language speakers; n = 69 German first language speakers; 5-point response scale from 1 ("completely agree") to 5 ("do not agree at all"); t-test for independent samples; case exclusion listwise; significance test two-sided at 5% level

	Women			Men			t-test			
	n	m	sd	n	m	sd	t	df	p	d
Occasional slaps are okay	67	4.54	0.927	28	4.04	1.232	2.8	93	0.032	0.49
	Non-German first language			German as first language			t-test			
	n	m	sd	n	m	sd	t	df	p	d
Prohibition of physical violence	31	1.1	0.301	64	1.6	1.022	3.24	82	0.002	0.25

of the use of physical violence in raising children than people with native German speakers (Table 11).

Parenting practices, such as the acceptance of physical punishment as a means of education, which parents had experienced as children, are not directly passed on from one generation to the next or transmitted within the cultural environment. Reflections on and rejections of such experienced parenting practices are reflected in the interviews, often based on cultural change due to the new environment:

"Because of our culture, we slap the children. Here we don't do that. Because we have been grown up like it, sometimes we do that." (Resident, 43, born and raised in Nigeria, English in the original)

[…] it wasn't my boys who had problems, but I had problems. I didn't know how to raise children, even though I am a preschool teacher. […] I got stuck between cultural boundaries. Many Pakistanis live here, and they do it very differently." (Resident 36, born and raised in Pakistan)

What is referred to here as "family" can also be associated with attributed functions of and in the family. Transferring duties which have for a long time been considered family duties to external institutions, such as the care and education of children, for instance, can greatly influence the understanding and the meaning of family (Wonneberger and Stelzig-Willutzki 2018). This is also evident in the topic of caring for the elderly: For many families, transferring care obligations to the state is not taken for granted, in some cases it is even unthinkable. In countries without social welfare systems, the family often represents the only care system (BMFSFJ 2010a). Although it is common in Germany today to outsource traditional family functions such as the care of senior citizens, the normative beliefs in this regard are relatively stable and strongly depend on the family's cultural background: About 98 percent of the people of Turkish descent are cared for at home compared to 73 percent of people with no migratory background (Budde 2018). Instead of traditional forms of elder-care, Germany is apparently characterized by a form of social care today which is often perceived as alienating and undignified by families of Turkish descent. Not being cared for in old age by relatives can also be associated with great shame, because normative believes and practices differ from each other (Läsker and Yortanli 2012). Although this topic was not studied in greater depth, some interviews statements show that this also applies to "western-oriented" residents from countries with a poorer social security system in old age (USA) and cannot generally and necessarily be derived from a cultural background which is considered more family-centered. For example, a resident who returned from the USA after 40 years to care for her mother in Germany explains:

> "[…] I came here because of my mother. Because I am the only child, and there was no one else, and then I thought. I thought about it for over a year and thought, my mother, she really needs me, because there is no one for her here." (Woman, approx. 80 years, born and raised in Germany, lived in the USA for 40 years)

Caring and being cared for are functions that are strongly associated with families (Wonneberger and Stelzig-Willutzki 2018). The perceptions of when the conditions for adequate care are sufficient are changing (among others Kaufmann 1990). This is also viewed differently by the residents of the housing estate, as their attitudes towards necessary requirements for "good" parenthood shows. The residents were asked what "conditions" should be met to have children" (cf. Diabaté and Lück 2014). There are no differences in terms of gender, age, and first languages. The comparative role model study by Diabaté et al. (2016) also shows hardly any differences between Turkish and German speaking respondents: Both most people with a Turkish and people with no migratory background held the opinion that women should have gained a foothold in their profession, regardless of whether her partner is employed or not. However, the rate of approval to this statement is significantly higher for women than men in both groups. One explanation for this finding might be that young Turkish women place more emphasis on autonomy than older generations due to their good education, and these differences also hide economic aspects (Diabaté et al. 2016). The following section deals with further role models.

6 Attitudes Towards Gender Role Models

Gender role models, i.e. beliefs about the sexual division of labor between women and men in the family, are particularly important for the study of family role models (cf. Pfau-Effinger 2004, p. 82). Based on this principle, the last section of the Lenzsiedlung survey dealt with the residents' ideas about the allocation of roles between men and women in the family. Figure 7 illustrates that all respondents clearly favor an egalitarian division of labor.

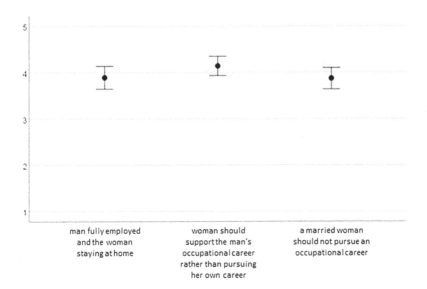

Fig. 7 Labor division: "What are your ideas about the labor division between man and woman?" (n = 107, response scale: 1 = "completely agree" to 5 = "do not agree at all"; arithmetic mean and confidence interval of the arithmetic mean); scale based on Statistisches Bundesamt and Wissenschaftszentrum Berlin für Sozialforschung (2018). *Source*: figure created by the authors

The comparison of different groups in terms of gender, first language (non-German and German, Turkish and German) does not reveal any relevant differences.

Overall, a higher level of education coincides with egalitarian attitudes, but egalitarian attitudes have gained in importance over time across all educational groups, as the 2018 data report shows (Statistisches Bundesamt and Wissenschaftszentrum Berlin für Sozialforschung 2018). Not the cultural background alone seems to be decisive for one's attitude towards the mother's role, but education seems to play a crucial role. Gebel and Heyne (2017) point out that while there is a higher rejection of working mothers in the so-called MENA countries (Middle East and North Africa), there are also different views within the MENA states regarding mothers' employment. Therefore, a differentiated view seems to be necessary in this respect. In this context, education is discussed as the decisive factor for shaping one's attitude towards mothers' employment (Gebel and Heyne 2017). However, this item was not part of our standardized survey.

The variable "age" suggests differences in answers to the question "what are your ideas about the labor division between men and women?", even if no systematic trend can be identified: The 41- to 50-year-old respondents in the housing estate reject the idea that it "is much better for all people involved" if "the man is fully employed and the woman stays at home and takes care of the household and the children" (i.e., a traditional attitude) much more strongly by than any other age group. Again, it is the middle age group that holds a less conservative role model regarding the division of labor in families than younger and older generations.

A comparing look at the 2018 data report shows that overall, it is rather the younger people who are more egalitarian in terms of ideas about gender roles than older people. Egalitarian attitudes have increased for both men and women in Germany over the years. However, the repeatedly discussed differences between West and East Germany with its orientation towards the ideal of both parents working also persist. In relation to the entire population in Germany, women express slightly more egalitarian attitudes towards labor division than men. They also perceive the consequences working mothers might have for their children as less negative (Statistisches Bundesamt and Wissenschaftszentrum Berlin für Sozialforschung 2018).

Although no major differences in the attitudes towards women's and men's roles can be found in the Lenzsiedlung survey, there is evidence that the experiences of girls and boys growing up might differ. The guideline interviews reveal that many girls, especially from families with traditional gender role models, experience social control, surveillance, and numerous rules they must obey:

"We girls have to be careful what we do here. If a mother sees something she thinks is wrong, news spreads really quickly here, then it ends up at home and you are asked if it's true. [...] I know a few boys here, it's completely different for them. It's like boys can do that, girls can't. They can listen to music because they are boys, so the parents don't care. Mothers think that we girls always have to be polite, always well dressed, always respectful. My mother also always says, be careful how you are here, it can spread quickly. [Resident, 16 years old, parents are from Turkey]

In addition to general gender norms and ideas of what girls and boys "usually" do and how they should present themselves, "safety" is mentioned as another factor why younger children and girls should not go around the neighborhood unrestrictedly. Older boys, however, seem to be able to move relatively "freely" in the neighborhood. Differences in gender roles therefore seem to be established in early age, although the occurrence and effects in relation to family life would need to be examined more closely.

7 Results from the Guideline Interviews on the Everyday Life of Mothers and Fathers in Families

Although the standardized survey shows hardly any differences in attitudes towards women's and men's roles, an egalitarian division of labor between the genders in the families of the housing estate seems to be an exception, if two partners are present at all. In this context, the guideline interviews reveal further factors that were not inquired in the standardized survey: In addition to traditional views learnt through socialization within one's family of origin, state incentives such as the splitting of income between spouses and free co-insurance with the usually male breadwinner are likely to promote a traditional gender division of labor, especially for economically weaker families. The current division of labor in families, as in the German society as a whole (Statistisches Bundesamt and Wissenschaftszentrum Berlin für Sozialforschung 2018), is still less egalitarian compared to the expressed attitudes.

The guideline interviews suggest that in the Lenzsiedlung a lower educational status coincides with a stronger adherence to the pattern of the conventional nuclear family with a gender-differentiated division of labor. This finding seems true for all respondents, no matter whether they have a German, Turkish or any other cultural background and even though the numerous single-parent families cannot always live up to this ideal.

Unlike women with a higher education or an academic degree, the attitude of "being in the comfortable situation not to have to work as a woman" due to the husband's high income could be more often observed among residents with a low education or no school degree. One resident of the latter category describes her situation as follows:

> "[...] now I am at home and as long as it is financially possible, I will stay at home with the little one. (...). If it should become tight, of course he has to go to daycare, and I have to start working again myself with [the man], right?" (Resident, 37, born and raised in Germany, three children, married to a man from Egypt)

The collected data also indicate that there are traditional everyday practices among people in partnerships where both partners come from a country with more traditional gender roles. In several cases, interviewees described how they adapt to the ideas of their more tradition-oriented partners, as the following quote illustrates:

> "With my parents, labor was divided. The one who came home earlier cleaned up or made food, and in my husband's family, the woman—his mother—did it. The husband actually didn't do anything [...]. I just accepted it because that's their culture, that the woman does everything." (Resident, 30 years, born and raised in Germany, two children, married to a man from Serbia).

In other cases, women with tradition-oriented partners—regardless of their cultural origin—seem to prefer a more equal life between men and women. The women recognize the importance of their own education, but cannot always implement it:

> "He told me... forget everything and start anew. And we have children. After that, you go to learn and so on. [...] And then four children and at the beginning no learning. No, you are not allowed! He can do everything, and I can do nothing. [...] So his parents with him. They say, he is a man, and you are a woman. Just like that. Because in his culture, you know, a woman is like this and man is like that. [...] but until now a man [makes a gesture of strength/determination] is a man and a woman is small. And I—no. And always I fight, always. I say, I fight for my children, too. Because, no matter what you do, you give everything to the children. [...] I must fight for my opinion. (Resident, late 20s, born and raised in Tunisia, five children, separated from her Tunisian husband)

Family in the Post-Migrant Society 133

According to a youth welfare worker in the district, it also happens that German men with more traditional views specifically look for women from more tradition-oriented countries to be able to enforce patriarchal power claims in the family:

> "[...] when German men have chosen foreign mothers, I say this deliberately, and then they were in such a patriarchal habitus in their relationships and conflicts arose from that. I've have experienced that with Asians, but also with Russian women. [...] Because there are power asymmetries in it, they are the sole earners, they have brought the woman to Germany, and now she must obey." (ASD worker in the district)

Therefore, while the collected data strongly indicate a tendency towards a more traditional division of labor between men and women, particularly in terms of employment, they also underline how important women are for social exchange and networking in the neighborhood. Especially mothers are very present in the housing estate; they seem to dominate mainly as social anchors and family managers. The guideline interviews provide numerous data illustrating this point. Data collected over two years of participant observation and informal conversations with the residents suggest that networks between families are established a lot more through mothers than through fathers, regardless of their cultural origin. The neighborhood networks of mothers obviously represent a particularly important resource.[6]

> "But that's generally the way it is here. Integration is female here, families, everything depends on the women." (Resident, early 50s, born and raised in Germany, two children, single parent)

Professionals from psychosocial counseling and social work also confirm this observation by stating that in many families, German as a foreign language is acquired faster by mothers than by fathers. Although mothers are generally less likely to be employed and in two-parent families fathers are often the main breadwinners, fathers in the housing estate seem to learn German slower and not as well their female partners. Apart from the presumably better networking skills of

---

[6] This aspect, among others, has also been studied in the POMIKU project. A publication on the results of the egocentric network analysis with 50 people from the housing estate is under preparation.

mothers, the cost of German classes, which only fathers with an income must pay for, is another possible explanation for this:

> "I have talked about the fact that I would like to see fathers in these families to set out to learn better German. There are programs. They would have been basically ready to attend, but it failed because, if you work, you earn money, and then you have to pay for these courses by yourself at some point. So the question is, do I want to spend 500 euros. [...] Who am I to tell them, you have to invest that money now? At that point I thought that it would be great if these language courses would be offered for free to all who are willing to learn German." (Educational counselor)

Moreover, many men with a migratory background in the housing estate work in low-skilled jobs where German language skills are not very important. However, when it comes to language, it should not be forgotten that families with little social interaction are probably underrepresented in the study and that interviews with men were missing in the evaluation. Furthermore, no information can be given at this point on the extent to which women or mothers might also be excluded from language classes and integration in the housing estate. However, there are indicators for this assumption:

> "Sometimes there are also [segregated] groups, but I think that is because many Turkish women can't speak German, not because they don't accept the others, but because they can't communicate. Then they stick to themselves." (Resident, 53, born and raised in Turkey)
> "...they are always among themselves. I would probably do the same if I were abroad, that I would first look for people who speak German. But I notice that they are not so willing to integrate." (Resident, 75 years old, born and raised in Germany)

If one disregards these assumptions and picks up on the existing findings, they clearly contradict numerous results of previous studies, according to which men with a migratory background try more to be involved in raising children than would be considered "normal" in their country of origin and more than the previous generation. They also take over the role of the family representative in public. This higher involvement of fathers with a migratory background in everyday family life compared to mothers has often been observed before. It is generally attributed to better German skills and a more dominant role of the father in the family compared to German families (BMFSFJ 2010b). How can these large differences between our own findings and the results of other studies be explained? Although there is no conclusive answer, striking are the close networks of many residents within the housing state, which have been mentioned before. These networks might also lead to a stronger participation in family-related services, regardless of whether families have a migratory background or not. Someone who is approached by a neighbor, "taken along" and profits from his or her knowledge, might participate much easier than someone in a more anonymous residential neighborhood:

> "[...] when we go to the playground, because you know so many people, you know, there is always an eye, if I am also busy with the little one, I can breastfeed her in peace, because I know there are enough mothers, they know each other and they would help in an emergency, if she falls. Or also, recently, a boy fell at the skate park, no one knew him, but there were people who helped him. He was taken care of, and an ambulance was called, so you can see that even if you don't know them, help is provided here." (Resident, 30 years old, born and raised in Germany).

8 Conclusion

This study of large high-rise housing estate demonstrates that the question of "cultural" family role models which are often described as characteristic for certain societies, regions, generations, or social milieus, can only be answered in a differentiated way if further categories are taken into account. Family life in the neighborhood is extremely diverse, but the ideas of what makes a "good" family life are not as different across the groups analyzed as one might expect from a population from over 60 countries of origin.

Particularly the question of what exactly "family" means (topic one) is generally answered with a high level of agreement: The presence of at least two generations (parent/s and child/ren) forming a social unit makes a designation as "family" more likely than a partnership without children. As far as the importance of biological-genetic kinship relationships ("blood relationship") as a marker of "family" is concerned, differences between the interview partners became visible; however, based on the open guideline interviews a systematic correlation between the variety of attitudes and the cultural origin cannot be established ad hoc. People with a non-German first language seem to hold a slightly more conservative family role model, but Turkish native speakers do not seem to be more conservative than German native speakers. Marriage also does not seem to play a special role for native Turkish speaking respondents.

As was to be expected, a rather conservative family role model, based on the traditional image of the nuclear family, is found among older residents, who were strongly socialized with the ideal of the bourgeois nuclear family. Surprisingly, however, younger respondents also expressed similar attitudes. This result corresponds with the postulate of current studies that for today's younger generation family formation is strongly associated with the desire for stability and security in relationships (Albert et al. 2019). Even if the traditional nuclear family itself is not a guarantee for stable family relationships, it is apparently still often associated with it.

There seem to be no major differences in the housing estate concerning the question of the role distribution between men and women (topic three). Again, however—besides the older generation—it is the younger residents who seem to hold a slightly more conservative ideal regarding the division of labor in families than the middle age group. However, differences in experience become apparent when the upbringing of girls and boys is compared, as the explorative interviews show. Moreover, the involvement in neighborhood networks and educational institutions differs in terms of gender but does barely correlate with people's cultural origin.

More obvious differences emerge in the ideas about the function of the family (topic two). Particularly between native German and Turkish speakers, there are several differences. These become obvious first and foremost regarding the importance of children. While some explanations emphasize a generally stronger family focus in families of Turkish descent, others offer different explanations. The experience, for instance, that older citizens are not necessarily cared for and supported by their children, but that the state will take over this responsibility, if necessary, might be obvious for parents with a German background, but the first generation of Turkish-born parents will hardly have grown up with this experience.

Turkish-speakers, compared to German-speaking parents, also see themselves more responsible for providing their children with a larger variety of leisure activities and playing with them instead of other children. They also agree more with the statement that it is fun to have children in the household and to watch them grow up than respondents of German descent. A similar picture emerges around the topic of parents' duties in supporting their children: Turkish-speaking respondents regard parents as more liable to promote their children's academic performance than German native speakers. They also hold parents more responsible for poor school performance than German native speakers. This finding is further underlined by the fact that respondents of Turkish descent agree to a larger degree than German speakers with the statement that daycare offers children fewer opportunities for personal development than the family. Apart from "school performance", "diligence" and "obedience" are major educational goals where the ideas between Turkish and German speaking respondents differ: The former regard all those values as more important than the latter.

Taken together, these differences between Turkish and German speaking respondents could be interpreted in one way: For a long time, families in Germany have been dependent on their own resources in terms of their children's educational concerns and academic support. People who moved to Germany as foreign workers with low education, including many immigrants from Turkey and their children and grandchildren, who were born in Germany, were and are facing multiple challenges due to their own educational biographies. Their trust in the German state which provides daycare facilities and school education for their children—services which have been gradually expanded to all-day care and schooling in recent years—may therefore not have grown at the same pace as that of German parents, particularly after decades of experiencing disadvantages in Germany.

From all differences between the various groups that have been analyzed so far two aspects stand out with regards to the central question: Firstly, the younger age group, regardless of their descent, holds rather conservative family and gender role models. This is also underlined by the fact that this group considers the educational goal "obedience" most important. Secondly, differences between Turkish and German speaking respondents stand out in terms of how important they regard children and parents' responsibilities in the family. However, even between these two groups, the similarities in their family role models are greater than their differences.

It can be concluded that the characteristic "cultural background" is only one category among many others which shape the nature of family role models in different groups of residents who live in a post-migrant society such as Germany in 2021. It must also be viewed in a differentiated way. This is not to deny or ignore the fact that many people who themselves or whose ancestors, partners, or family members have immigrated to Germany have been and often still are confronted with numerous problems today. However, the differences found regarding family images and role models in the sample does not seem to go along the boundary between people "with" and "without" a migratory background. They are at least co-determined by other characteristics such as age, gender, living environment, neighborhood, community, and education. These factors probably also affect the normative family and gender role models. It can be assumed that ideas of a way of life not only influence how people live and behave, but they are also vice versa shaped by everyday practices: The existing forms of social relationships, however they have come into existence, also forms family images and role models, and thus values and norms.

The social sciences have predicted a gradual (one-sided) assimilation of family role models regarding cultural background or migration experience even before the term "post-migrant society" started to dominate professional discourses. Diabaté et al. (2016) classified the results of their study of family role models of Turkish and German adolescents as follows:

"Socialization through the German (educational) system and increased contacts with peers and life partners with no migratory background will lead to a convergence of family role models over the following generations (Gründler 2012). People of Turkish descent will continue to adapt to the family role models of the majority society through their integration." (ibid., p. 17)

However, it should not be overlooked that there might be numerous groups in the housing estate which could not have been accessed during the research project and have thus remained invisible due to language problems or personal reservations. It is possible that some residents feel unsettled when the diversity of family forms and norms are studied in their immediate vicinity and tend to strengthen their own attitudes in an attempt to distance themselves from others. Therefore, numerous questions remain open at this point: How exactly do attitudes and norms about family life in a neighborhood which is characterized by dense social networks influence each other? What influence does the daily confrontation with different family forms have on one's own convictions regarding family role models? Which mechanisms help to expand individual family role models and which ones solidify existing normative beliefs through processes of demarcation?

References

AID: A. 2019. Aufwachsen in Deutschland 2019. Alltagswelten von Kindern, Jugendlichen und Familien. Der neue DJI-Survey. https://surveys.dji.de/index.php?m=msg,0&fID=20. Accessed 13 Sept 2021.

Albert, Matthias, Klaus Hurrelmann, and Gudrun Quenzel. 2019. 18. SHELL JUGENDSTUDIE. JUGEND 2019. Eine Generation meldet sich zu Wort. Hamburg: Deutsche Shell Holding GmbH.

Allgemeine Bevölkerungsumfrage der Sozialwissenschaften (ALLBUS). https://www.gesis.org/allbus/allbus. Accessed 31 Aug 2021.

Autorengruppe Bildungsberichterstattung. 2020. Bildung in Deutschland 2020. Ein indikatorengestützter Bericht mit einer Analyse zu Bildung in einer digitalisierten Welt. https://www.bildungsbericht.de/static_pdfs/bildungsbericht-2020.pdf. Accessed 31 Aug 2021.

Bertram, Hans, ed. 1991. *Die Familie in Westdeutschland. Stabilität und Wandel familialer Lebensformen.* Deutsches Jugend-Institut Familien-Survey Book Series (DJIFAM, Vol. 1). Opladen: Leske + Budrich.

BiB (Bundesinstitut für Bevölkerungsforschung). 2013. *Familien Leitbilder: Vorstellungen, Meinungen, Erwartungen.* Wiesbaden: Bundesinstitut für Bevölkerungsforschung.
BiB (Bundesinstitut für Bevölkerungsforschung). 2017. *Familien Leitbilder: Alles wie gehabt? Partnerschaft und Elternschaft in Deutschland.* Wiesbaden: Bundesinstitut für Bevölkerungsforschung.
BMFSFJ. 2021. Neunter Familienbericht. Eltern sein in Deutschland. Zusammenfassung des Gutachtens der Sachverständigenkommission. https://www.bmfsfj.de/bmfsfj/ministerium/berichte-der-bundesregierung/neunter-familienbericht. Accessed 31 Aug 2021.
BMFSFJ. 2016. Migration und Familie. Kindheit mit Zuwanderungshintergrund. Gutachten des Wissenschaftlichen Beirats für Familienfragen beim Bundesministerium für Familie, Senioren, Frauen und Jugend. Short version. https://www.bmfsfj.de/resource/blob/83738/889bf8299d1ca2d70ec8a271113aaba8/kurzfassung-migration-und-familie-2016-data.pdf. Accessed 1 July 2021.
BMFSFJ. 2010a. Das Wohlbefinden von Eltern. Monitor Familienforschung. Beiträge aus Forschung, Statistik und Familienpolitik. Issue 22. https://www.bmfsfj.de/resource/blob/76210/0566107981a86ac4693cadf9a708967b/monitor-2010-03-data.pdf. Accessed 31 Aug 2021.
BMFSFJ. 2010b. Ehe, Familie, Werte – Migrantinnen und Migranten in Deutschland. Monitor Familienforschung. Beiträge aus Forschung, Statistik und Familienpolitik, Issue 24. https://www.bmfsfj.de/resource/blob/76216/2aeaddc89821f9a2627bf454bc7c8893/monitor-familienforschung-nr-24-data.pdf. Accessed 31 Aug 2021.
Broden, Anne, and Paul Mecheril, eds. 2007. Re-Präsentationen. Dynamiken der Migrationsgesellschaft, Düsseldorf: in-house publisher. https://www.ida-nrw.de/publikationen/reader-buecher/detail/re-praesentationen-dynamiken-der-migrationsgesellschaft. Accessed 28 Oct 2021.
Budde, Svenja. 2018. Ältere Menschen mit Migrationsgeschichte: gesundheitliche Lage und Zugang zu Gesundheitsförderung und Versorgung. https://www.lzg.nrw.de/_php/login/dl.php?u=/_media/pdf/service/Veranst/180307_vernetzung/budde_aeltere_menschen_07-03-2018.pdf. Accessed 29 June 2019.
de Moll, Frederick, Stefanie Bischoff, Karoline Kruczynski, Margaret Pardo-Puhlmann, and Tanja Betz. 2016. Projekt Educare: Skalendokumentation zur Elternbefragung an Kindertageseinrichtungen. Goethe-University Frankfurt am Main. https://www.allgemeine-erziehungswissenschaft.uni-mainz.de/files/2019/07/EDUCARE_Skalendoku_Elternbefragung_KiTa.pdf. Accessed 31 Aug 2021.
DJI. 2014. Survey Datenbank des Deutschen Jugendinstituts. https://www.dji.de/ueber-uns/projekte/projekte/survey-datenbank.html. Accessed 13 Sept 2021.
Diabaté, Sabine, and Detlev Lück. 2014. Familienleitbilder – Identifikation und Wirkungsweise auf generatives Verhalten. *Zeitschrift Für Familienforschung* 26 (1): 49–69.
Diabaté, Sabine, Samira Beringer, and Yannik Garcia Ritz. 2016. Ähnlicher als man denkt?! – Ein Vergleich der Familienleitbilder von Personen mit türkischem und ohne Migrationshintergrund in Deutschland. *Bevölkerungsforschung Aktuell* 2: 13–19.
Esser, Hartmut. 1990. „Habits", „Frames" und „Rational Choice". Die Reichweite von Theorien der rationalen Wahl (am Beispiel der Erklärung des Befragtenverhaltens). *Zeitschrift für Soziologie* 19(4):231–247.

Foroutan, Naika, Coşkun Canan, Benjamin Schwarze, Steffen Beigang, Sina Arnold, and Dorina Kalkum. 2014. *Hamburg postmigrantisch. Einstellungen der Hamburger Bevölkerung zu Musliminnen und Muslimen in Deutschland*. Berlin: Berliner Institut für empirische Integrations- und Migrationsforschung.

Gebel, Michael, and Stefanie Heyne. 2017. *Familienverständnis in Nordafrika und dem Nahen Osten. Analysen zu familiären Rollen und zur Abgrenzung vom Staat*. Bamberg: University of Bamberg Press.

Gerlach, Irene. 2017. Familienpolitik in der Bundesrepublik. Kleine Politikfeldgeschichte. *Aus Politik und Zeitgeschichte (APuZ)* 30/31:16–21.

Giesel, Katharina. 2007. *Leitbilder in den Sozialwissenschaften. Begriffe, Theorien und Forschungskonzepte*. Wiesbaden: VS Verlag | Springer Fachmedien.

Gründler, Sabine. 2012. *Partnerschaftszufriedenheit von Deutschen und türkischen Migranten. Der Einfluss soziologischer und sozialpsychologischer Determinanten auf Partnerschaften*. Wiesbaden: VS Verlag | Springer Fachmedien.

Janßen, Andrea, and Ayça Polat. 2006. Soziale Netzwerke türkischer Migrantinnen und Migranten. *Aus Politik und Zeitgeschichte (APuZ)* 1 & 2:11–17.

Kaufmann, Franz-Xaver. 1990. *Zukunft der Familie. Stabilität, Stabilitätsrisiken und Wandel der familialen Lebensformen sowie ihre gesellschaftlichen und politischen Bedingungen*. München: Beck.

Keller, Carsten. 2015. Problemviertel? Imageproduktion und soziale Benachteiligung städtischer Quartiere. https://www.bpb.de/politik/innenpolitik/gangsterlaeufer/202834/problemviertel-image-und-benachteiligung12.5.2015%20I%20Von:%20Carsten%20Keller. Accessed 28 Oct 2021.

Kohn, Melvin L. 1959. Social Class and Parental Values. *American Journal of Sociology* 64: 337–351.

Kohn, Melvin L. 1969. *Class and Conformity. A Study in Values*. Homewood: Dorsey Press.

Kohn, Melvin L., and Carrie Schoenbach. 1986. Social Stratification and Parental Values: A Multi-national Assessment. *Sociological Forum* 1 (1): 73–101.

Koppetsch, Cornelia. 2014. Die Wiederkehr der Konformität? Wandel der Mentalitäten – Wandel der Generationen. Bundeszentrale für politische Bildung, eds. *Aus Politik und Zeitgeschichte* 64(49):37–43.

Läsker, Anna, and Pinar Yortanli. 2012. Alt werden in der Migration. In *Alter(n) bewegt*, ed. Gabriele Kleiner, 157–167. Wiesbaden: VS Verlag.

Lenze, Anne. 2021. *Alleinerziehende weiter unter Druck. Bedarfe, rechtliche Regelungen und Reformansätze*. Gütersloh: Bertelsmann Stiftung.

Lenze, Anne, and Antje Funcke. 2016. *Alleinerziehende unter Druck. Rechtliche Rahmenbedingungen, finanzielle Lage und Reformbedarf*. Gütersloh: Bertelsmann Stiftung.

Lück, Detlev, and Sabine Diabaté. 2015. Familienleitbilder. Ein theoretisches Konzept. In *Familienleitbilder in Deutschland. Kulturelle Vorstellungen zu Partnerschaft, Elternschaft und Familienleben*. Eds. Norbert F. Schneider, Sabine Diabaté, and Kerstin Ruckdeschel, 19–28. Opladen: Budrich – (Beiträge zur Bevölkerungswissenschaft 48).

Lück, Detlev, Sabine Diabaté, and Kerstin Ruckdeschel. 2017. Cultural Conceptions of Family as Inhibitors of Change in Family Lives: The ‚Leitbild' Approach. In *Family Continuity and Change. Contemporary European Perspectives*, eds. Vida Česnuitytė, Detlev Lück, and Eric D. Widmer, 61–86. London: Palgrave Macmillan.

Pardo-Puhlmann, Margaret, Stefanie Bischoff, and Tanja Betz. 2016. *Leitbilder. Systematisierungen und begriffliche Klärungen aus sozialwissenschaftlicher Perspektive*. Frankfurt a. M.: Goethe University.
Peuckert, Rüdiger. 2012. Ein-Eltern-Familien (Alleinerziehende): Randgruppe, „neues" familiales Selbstverständnis oder „ganz normale" Familienform? In *Familienformen im sozialen Wandel*, ed. Rüdiger Peuckert, 345–379. Wiesbaden: VS Verlag.
Pfau-Effinger, Birgit. 2004. Historical Paths of the Male Breadwinner Family Model – Explanation for Cross-national Differences. *British Journal for Sociology* 55 (3): 377–399.
Schenk, Liane Alexandra, and Monika Habermann. 2020. *Migration und Alter*. Berlin: De Gruyter.
Schneider, Norbert F., Sabine Diabaté, and Kerstin Ruckdeschel. 2015. *Familienleitbilder in Deutschland. Kulturelle Vorstellungen zu Partnerschaft, Elternschaft und Familienleben*. Opladen: Budrich – (Beiträge zur Bevölkerungswissenschaft, 48).
Schneider, Norbert F., and Sabine Diabaté. 2020. Familienleitbilder. In *Handbuch Familie*, ed. Jutta Ecarius and Anja Schierbaum, 345–379. Wiesbaden: VS Verlag.
Schneider, Norbert F. 2008. Grundlagen der sozialwissenschaftlichen Familienforschung – Einführende Betrachtungen. In *Lehrbuch Moderne Familiensoziologie*, ed. Norbert F. Schneider, 9–21. Opladen: Budrich.
Statistikamt Nord. 2021. Population and social data of the Statistical Area 39010. Unpublished data, 31. December 2020.
Statistisches Bundesamt. 2019. Bevölkerung und Erwerbstätigkeit. Bevölkerung mit Migrationshintergrund – Ergebnisse des Mikrozensus 2018. Wiesbaden. 62. https://www.destatis.de/DE/Themen/Gesellschaft-Umwelt/Bevoelkerung/Migration-Integration/Publikationen/Downloads-Migration/migrationshintergrund-2010220187004.pdf?__blob=publicationFile. Accessed 31 Aug 2021.
Statistisches Bundesamt. 2018. Bevölkerung und Erwerbstätigkeit. Bevölkerung mit Migrationshintergrund – Ergebnisse des Mikrozensus 2017. Wiesbaden. 4. https://www.destatis.de/DE/Themen/Gesellschaft-Umwelt/Bevoelkerung/Migration-Integration/Publikationen/Downloads-Migration/migrationshintergrund-2010220177004.pdf?__blob=publicationFile&v=4#page=4. Accessed 31 Aug 2021.
Statistisches Bundesamt (Destatis) and Wissenschaftszentrum Berlin für Sozialforschung (WZB), eds. 2018. In cooperation with the Socio-Economic Panel (SOEP) and the Deutsches Institut für Wirtschaftsforschung (DIW Berlin) 2018. Datenreport 2018. Ein Sozialbericht für die Bundesrepublik Deutschland. Chapter 10.2. Bundeszentrale für politische Bildung (bpb). file:///C:/Users/sabin/AppData/Local/Temp/dr2018_bf_mit_korrekturseite_142_200525.pdf. Accessed 28 Oct 2021.
Weber, Florian. 2013. Zur Problematisierung „kultureller Differenzierungen" in der quartiersbezogenen Stadtpolitik „Soziale Stadt". In *Migrationsort Quartier. Zwischen Segregation, Integration und Interkultur*, eds. Olaf Schnur, Philipp Zakrzewski, and Matthias Drilling, 55–74. Wiesbaden: VS Verlag I Springer Fachmedien.
Will, Anne-Kathrin. 2020. Migrationshintergrund – Wieso, woher, wohin? BpB (2020). https://www.bpb.de/gesellschaft/migration/laenderprofile/304523/migrationshintergrund#footnode15-15. Accessed 31 Aug 2021.

Wonneberger, Astrid, and Sabina Stelzig-Willutzki. 2018. Familie. In *Familienwissenschaft. Grundlagen und Überblick*, eds. Astrid Wonneberger, Katja Weidtmann, and Sabina Stelzig-Willutzki, 489–512. Wiesbaden: VS Verlag l Springer Fachmedien.

Dr. Sabina Stelzig *Department of Social Work, HAW Hamburg*
After completing her doctorate degree in Sociology on the topic of women's migration, Dr. Sabina Stelzig worked as a research assistant and lecturer in family and migration studies at the University of Hamburg and the Hamburg Institute of International Economics (HWWI). In 2012 she became involved in the development of the Master's program in Applied Family Sciences at the University of Applied Sciences (HAW) Hamburg, where she also teaches Sociology and empirical research methods in the BA Social Work. Since 2018, she has been part of the research team in the BMBF project POMIKU on "post-migrant family cultures".

Prof. Dr. Katja Weidtmann *Department of Social Work, HAW Hamburg*
After her studies in Psychology and Child and Adolescent Psychiatry at the University of Hamburg, Katja Weidtmann worked as a research assistant at the Medical Faculty and at the Clinic for Child and Adolescent Psychiatry, Psychotherapy and Psychosomatics of the University Medical Center Hamburg-Eppendorf. Here she also received her doctorate with an evaluation study of the special outpatient clinic "Giftedness Center". After working as a school psychologist in Lower Saxony and in Hamburg and in a practice for child and adolescent psychiatry and psychotherapy, she became a research assistant at the University of Applied Sciences (HAW) Hamburg in 2012, helped to establish the Master's program in Applied Family Sciences and has been a professor for Family Psychology and Family Counseling since 2016. She is also the head of the Master's program in Applied Family Sciences and of the research project POMIKU.

Printed in the USA
CPSIA information can be obtained
at www.ICGtesting.com
CBHW020814151024
15807CB00022B/105